A PRIMER OF
POLITICAL ANALYSIS

A PRIMER OF POLITICAL ANALYSIS
Second Edition

D. A. Strickland
L. L. Wade
R. E. Johnston

Markham Publishing Company/Chicago

MARKHAM POLITICAL SCIENCE SERIES

Aaron Wildavsky, Editor

Axelrod, *Conflict of Interest: A Theory of Divergent Goals with Applications to Politics*
Barber, *Citizen Politics: An Introduction to Political Behavior,* Second Edition
Barber, ed., *Power to the Citizen: Introductory Readings*
Barber, ed., *Readings in Citizen Politics: Studies of Political Behavior*
Cnudde and Neubauer, eds., *Empirical Democratic Theory*
Coplin, *Introduction to International Politics: A Theoretical Overview*
Coplin, ed., *Simulation in the Study of Politics*
Coplin and Kegley, eds., *A Multi-method Introduction to International Politics: Observation, Explanation, and Prescription*
Dolbeare and Dolbeare, *American Ideologies: The Competing Political Beliefs of the 1970s*
Dvorin, ed., *The Senate's War Powers: Debate on Cambodia from the Congressional Record*
Greenstein, *Personality and Politics: Problems of Evidence, Inference, and Conceptualization*
Greenstein and Lerner, eds., *A Source Book for the Study of Personality and Politics*
Lane, *Political Thinking and Consciousness: The Private Life of the Political Mind*
Lyden and Miller, eds., *Planning-Programming-Budgeting: A Systems Approach to Management,* Second Edition
McDonald, *Party Systems and Elections in Latin America*
Mitchell, *Public Choice in America: An Introduction to American Government*
Mitchell, *Why Vote?*
Payne, *The American Threat: The Fear of War As an Instrument of Foreign Policy*
Ranney, ed., *Political Science and Public Policy*
Ross, *American National Government: An Introduction to Political Institutions*
Ross, ed., *Public Choice and Public Policy: Seven Cases in American Government*
Ross and Mitchell, eds., *Introductory Readings in American Government: A Public Choice Perspective*
Russett, ed., *Economic Theories of International Politics*
Sharkansky, *Public Administration: Policy-Making in Government Agencies,* Second Edition
Sharkansky, ed., *Policy Analysis in Political Science*
Strickland, Wade, and Johnston, *A Primer of Political Analysis,* Second Edition

Copyright © 1968, 1972 by Markham Publishing Company
All rights reserved
Printed in U.S.A.
Library of Congress Catalog Card Number: 79-174990
Paperback Standard Book Number: 8410-3064-2
Clothbound Standard Book Number: 8410-3083-9

224271

FOREWORD

In such a rapidly moving field of intellectual activity as modern political science, there are not enough *primers* to provide up-to-date basic information or to supply alternative introductions adapted to the several audiences who may be interested in the subject. This *Primer* is a sophisticated guide to the ways of thinking that "decision" analysts, including game theorists, have disseminated among professional students of politics.

The reader will be gratified to find that he is spared a routine description of the skin and bones of government. The *Primer* provides a living image of politics that deals with fundamental notions of structure and function. Hence, the attentive reader is gradually equipped to perceive with understanding, even with excitement, the complex connections that may be discerned when even the driest official skin or the most commonplace formal bone is properly defined.

The *Primer* introduces exercises in thinking about how to derive theorems about politics from the principal definitions in the book. There is also a selection of problems chosen to give meaning to each expository essay and to arouse problem-oriented involvement on the reader's part.

Would I write a different primer? This, by the way, is surely a question that every reader will find himself challenged to raise. If he would not do it somewhat differently, the *Primer* would be less successfully evocative than it is.

Harold D. Lasswell

PREFACE

*Nitimur in vetitum semper
cupimusque negata. . . .*
(We always strive for what is forbidden
and desire what we are denied. . . .)

—Ovid, *Amores,* III, 4, 17

This book is intended as a primer for the analysis of political behavior. It is meant to provide the student with concepts and methods that will apply to *any* political system. It should enable him to handle college materials on politics and government with more economy, lucidity, and logical force than he can acquire through the traditional textbooks, many of which are still dominated by a descriptive or a doctrinal bias. Our ambition here is to contribute something to the disproof of Schumpeter's dictum which says that

. . . the typical citizen drops down to a lower level of mental performance as soon as he enters the political field. . . . He becomes a primitive again [*Capitalism, Socialism, and Democracy*].

Some readers will find our approach radical—not in terms of the present thinking of political scientists (which it merely reflects and simplifies), but in terms of its departure from the textbook emphasis on citizenship, offices, procedures, and institutions. We do not start with the traditional debate over good and bad forms of government. It is our conviction that students *cannot* become good citizens until they learn to think clearly about public policy, until they can think the issues all the way through, and until they come to appreciate the thinking, the assumptions, and even the illogicalities of their fellow citizens. Then and only then is it time to ask questions about the best forms of government, the basic rights and duties of men, and the standards for judging political behavior.

Next to understanding the difference between *blaming* and *explaining,* the most important thing to understand about modern political analysis is that there are two kinds of *causes* we look at in explaining political behavior. The one is the individual's *wants* or *intentions.* The other is the human *situation* at any particular time and place. On the one hand, everybody wants things and does things; and we can say that John Doe did *x* or failed to do *x.* On the other hand, when you add up all the things that everybody is doing, the sum may come out to be something that no one wants; so we can say that such-and-such is a very poor country, although everybody in it is trying hard to overcome its poverty. Just as it would be a mistake to blame you, the reader, for a crime someone else committed, so too it would be mistaken to blame the individuals in a political system for conditions they do not want and cannot presently change.

Thus, whether you take a relaxed or a very serious attitude toward morality, you have to determine the facts of the matter—*whether* something has happened that resembles a crime or a sin—before you can begin to discuss the ethical side of it. After determining the facts of the matter, you may typically feel that the moral issues are terribly complicated. We, on the other hand, typically feel that many moral questions are easy questions. As the theologian and aesthetician Vischer said: "What is moral is self-evident." The Biblical tradition is agreed on this and reduces ethics to the command to treat all other people the way you want to be treated, i.e., to help and not harm people (*Leviticus* 19:18; *Matthew* 22:39).

The present work is offered as a supplement and introduction to the texts now in use. Our approach consists of four elements.

1. *Definitions* are given. They are definitions of the concepts that are, at our present level of refinement, the most basic and

general in political science. They are stated in a way that is directly familiar to common sense and which refers directly to events and behavior in the everyday world.

2. *Examples* are given, showing how these definitions may be applied to experience.

3. *Sample Theorems* are presented. They are meant to be imitations of the proofs one might find, say, in plane geometry; and they are, of course, determined entirely by the assumptions and definitions we provide. Chapter 1 is a discussion of the set of reasonable assumptions about human political behavior that we employ in the theorems. These theorems are intended both to show how one can make logical deductions about political topics and to show that logic by itself is no better than the assumptions with which it begins. Hence, we offer proofs that contradict one another; the student and the teacher, working through these materials, will become more and more aware that it helps to think logically about politics and that it is absolutely necessary to begin with assumptions that are true in reality if one expects to arrive at a realistic conclusion.

4. *Problems* follow the sample theorems. They are, for the most part, taken from actual studies of political life. Moreover, they are problems that can be answered in a reasonable way by any sensible person who has read the earlier sections of the book. We do not provide a list of the "correct" answers: (a) because many of the problems require interpretive, essay responses where the best answer would be the fullest and most subtle one, and (b) because the teacher's learning and imagination could be short-circuited by our own, perhaps too narrow, conclusions.

The fruitfulness of any method in the social sciences lies wholly in its relation to clear, answerable questions about the world. Serious learning is therefore a matter of the precision and specification of *questions,* above all. Proving theories and selecting evidence to prove or disprove hypotheses are operations completely at the mercy of the quality of the formulated questions. Some questions, perhaps most, simply cannot ever be answered, because of the way in which they were *mis*formulated.

A typical misformulation of a question is to leave the key terms undefined. Another is to neglect to limit the scope of the question, so that a reasonable person would have a hard time imagining what kind of evidence could *possibly* be *ir*relevant to an answer. This latter error gobbles up human energy and results in most of the tragicomical little "dialogues" that make up our daily lives. It is easily corrected for by reversing the sense of the question or issue: if you notice that the *opposite* proposition makes equally good sense, probably the time has come to ask a better question.

Just as a faulty question cannot be answered, so a correct proof need not necessarily be true. You will notice that the proofs offered in this volume are formal rather than empirical in nature. This means that the content may or may not be true of the external world; *if* the assumptions are true, certain things follow logically. Proofs of this type most often employ the rules of deductive logic, although some very interesting ones can be constructed by the principle of exclusion, that is, by showing that of three possibilities the third *has* to be true because and only because the other two can be shown to be false.

These exercises are no mere intellectual game: they show us the way to more and more refined questions and answers about political life. They also contribute, by the precision they lend to our research and reasoning, to the selection of the best method-ologies for empirically proving theories. It would, for example, be dreadfully difficult to show whether a poverty program or a birth control policy achieved reasonable results for the money spent, without some skill in the area of formal proofs. Politi-cians, however, do not exactly emphasize this connection, for they have numerous motives for adopting policies and are not usually keen on having their alternatives limited or their mis-takes rigorously demonstrated.

Evidence that bears on the *empirical* proof of political propositions is unbelievably complex and confounded. Unlike lawyers, political scientists do not have well-established rules on the admissibility of evidence. In fact, every citizen in every political system seems to have his own favorite rules for crediting or discrediting facts. This little book was meant to steer clear of that morass. We mention a few illustrative cases without making any pretense of straying from the firm ground of formal analysis. Formal reasoning of the sort offered here is, on the other hand, a preparation—an intellectual conditioning—that helps people out of sloughs.

It cannot be stated too strongly, however, that whatever thinking is realistic and makes sense is a function of the world itself; you have to go out and look, and ask, and ponder it. What we *would like* to believe about politics is completely irrelevant to political fact. Both optimistic and cynical views of politics are true only when and if they *are* true, only if we know that this is the way the world really is and not the way we would like to think it is. The trouble with wishful thinking about politics is not so much that it does not work out very often—although that is true enough. The trouble is that it runs in one direction only: *if* you get other people to share your wishes, you will have them behaving the way you want. *But* it is easy to think, mistakenly, that they share your wishes *just because* they happen to be acting the way you would wish them to, or that all you have to do is *have* the wish and *it* will somehow find the people to share itself with you.

D.A.S.
L.L.W.
R.E.J.

NOTE TO
THE INSTRUCTOR

We share, as teachers of political science, the difficult task of interesting young students in the subject matter without at the same time encouraging their tendencies toward political dogmatism and irrationality. The main impediment here, in the opinion of your authors, is the imprecision of political language, which lends itself to misunderstandings, exaggerations, and mislocated passion. You may have felt, as we have, that a simplification of concepts would help all of us to build a better understanding and a saner political life.

The *Primer* is an effort to create a "standard grammar" of political analysis. It does not pretend to be the last word on concepts and methods; it is merely an invitation to the beginning student to put aside some of the emotional and judgmental baggage of his political experience for a while and to practice thinking more clearly and logically about politics. In our experience, the use of the book has helped students both to understand the substantive texts in political science and to perceive the subtleties of those texts better. In this respect, we recommend the *Primer* as a key to the standard texts. In other respects, it is useful as a guide to some of the basic relationships between our field and the other social sciences, for we try to define "conflict," "association," "system," and other concepts in a way that brings to the fore our common quest with the humanities, history, psychology, sociology, philosophy, and economics.

Responses to the first edition indicated to us that the utility of the *Primer* varies a great deal with the nature of the student clientele and with the theoretical position of the instructor. Some of our American and Canadian colleagues have liked the formalistic aspects of the book, while others have found this annoying. Still others liked the preparation it gives the student for analyzing empirical problems more clearly. In any case, we have found that students react even more diversely. Some have found it just what they wanted to straighten out their thinking and equip them for more efficient political thought and research, others have protested indignantly that there was nothing in the book they hadn't known already, and a few were profoundly disturbed that anyone would seek to apply the rationality of philosophy or economics to (of all things!) politics, asserting that the First Amendment protects them from having their political beliefs subjected to the tests of reason.

The technical question here, in view of our common interest in pedagogy, is how to handle such an instrument. Our best advice is to treat the entire book as a module comparable to the "wake up" exercises that used to be done in grammar schools at the beginning of the day. That is, we have found that the book will fairly rapidly bring the whole class up to a manageable level of sophistication if it is used selectively, giving due respect to the inobvious weaknesses and embarrassing little problems of each student. Thus, instead of going over each section of each chapter, it is preferable to encourage the students to discuss ideas and relations that they do not grasp or with which they do not agree. Then it is possible to monitor the progress of the class by having all the students write out answers to some of the "problems" which follow each chapter. In this fashion the particular deficiencies of each student will soon become visible, and can be dealt with more effectively.

Yet the *Primer* is intended to be more than a diagnostic device useful in correcting the thought habits of students in our field. It is also meant to awaken students to the fact that the better they understand their own political life the better they understand the world. This comparative and somewhat behavioralist approach also implies that there exist techniques and concepts which work in analyzing any and all political systems. That, along with our systems bias, implies further that the student can understand his own political position and his country only to the extent that he understands the political behavior of people elsewhere in the world and what they are doing about government. We use more comparative examples in this second edition because we have been finding that the present generation of students understands the importance of this approach intuitively, and they want more of it. It might even be said that the very idea of a "primer" in the field, or of a political "science" to begin with, carries with it a comparative perspective. Otherwise, we should have to write a series of primers, for example, *A Primer of Hindu Political Analysis.*

You may or may not agree with our theoretical biases and out metaphysical assumptions. That is half the fun. The discussion of the "assumptions" (in Chapter 1) can itself be a powerful pedagogical tool; and if you vary the assumptions and apply new ones to the later topics we will have achieved exactly what we wanted to achieve with this little book. That does not mean to encourage students to speculate endlessly about "what if . . ."— it means rather to urge the students to ask themselves "what if other people and political leaders believed . . ." (and somewhere no doubt they do believe that).

Because the *Primer* is an analytic tool, we expect that it too will be dismantled in the use. That is what it is for. We have pulled it apart in an attempt to improve it with this edition. We invite you to do the same in the course of teaching young people to think better about politics. Please let us know whether the glue holds, and if not, how to put the parts back together again.

The authors are especially grateful to Professor Roberta Steihm for a critique of this edition.

CONTENTS

	Foreword	v
	Preface	vii
	Note to the Instructor	xii
1	Assumptions	1
2	Political Systems	7
3	Decisions	30
4	Conflict	40
5	Conflict-Resolution	55
6	Opinion	65
7	Agency	85
8	Association	95
	Index	108

CHAPTER 1

Assumptions

Political science is the study of men related by authority. Put another way, it is the study of who says what the issues are, what is to be done about them, and by whom.

In recent years, political scientists have engaged in disputes as to whether one can *really* study politics scientifically. After reading this book, you will see that this is a rather foolish dispute. You may conclude that people should get on with the business of studying politics rather than fighting among themselves over the *only* way to do it.

The *political* scientists are, to be sure, convinced that the political *scientists* are going about it in the wrong manner; and vice versa. Actually, they are all probably doing scientific study because everyone is a scientist. All people (1) make observations, (2) try to find relationships among the things they observe, and (3) develop explanations and predictions (theories) about the world. That's all science is. It is *not* something mysterious and magical, possessed solely by people like geologists, chemists, psychiatrists, or even sociologists.

Of course, some persons are better scientists than others.

Some are able to sharpen and refine their explanations of the world by being very careful about *how* they collect and analyze their observations. Self-deception and limited experience may make their theories wrong. But to avoid these pitfalls, they just have to be very careful and logical about procedures and thinking.

It may also help to know that there is no such thing as "*the* scientific method." Any way you can get a handle on the world is a good way. If you study further in political and social science, you will hear terms like "survey research," "factor analysis," "regression analysis," and so forth. These are good methods and come in handy for certain kinds of problems. However, no particular method or technique is *the* scientific method. All that any of them can do is to organize your experiences (data) in such a way that you sometimes know more than you did before. One danger is to get so confused over *how* to study politics that you forget *why* and *what* you want to know. A lot of intelligent people do this.

Children are particularly good scientists. They love to explore the world and to seek reasons for what they see. Frequently, however, somebody gets embarrassed by such curiosity and tells them to "behave" and to accept, without looking at the evidence any further, other people's reasons rather than their own. This results in bad scientists.

When a scientist learns something new about the world or discovers that current theories are wrong, he is supposed to tell others *how* he found that out. Colleges and universities, conferences, learned journals, books, and casual conversations are the forums in which this is done. If you want to go very far into a subject you must therefore become acquainted with these forums.

In the course of your studies you will run up against the following questions: How can a person select the best theory if many people have different explanations of what is going on? The answer is that the prudent man will *temporarily* accept the theory that (1) has been written up so that intelligent people can understand it, without any mumbo-jumbo, (2) is expressed most simply and with a minimum of concepts, and (3) can explain more facts and observations. If you narrow the choice down to two theories which seem to explain the facts equally well, a good way of choosing the "best" is to use your artistic judgment—select the one you find most attractive. Or better yet, devise new techniques to show that one theory actually predicts better and/or explains more facts.

Another thing to remember is that old theories cannot always explain the new facts that inevitably crop up. This means two things: (1) all existing theories may be wrong, and (2) you should regard any theory as being, at best, only *probably* right. In fact the history of science is a graveyard of defunct, inadequate, and out-dated theories.

Everybody who watches television or reads the newspapers gets new facts about the political world. So what do we mean when we say in the Preface that one learns by going out and looking at politics? We mean that one should look at the behavior of leaders and followers in any human group, at numerous times, carefully, and with an open mind. When you *yourself* have made a number of observations and think you see some patterns of behavior, then you can attempt to explain why people behave in that way (and not in other ways).

Political figures behave by making rules which they want others to obey. You can go and find out who makes the rules, what rules they make, who obeys them, who does not, what happens to those who do and do not obey, whether the rules are changed, by whom, and so on. You know already how to look for some of these things. The more clearly you can see them and the more of them you can see, the easier it will be to explain *why* they happen that way.

Just looking at the political world will not, however, be the same as understanding it. To understand it, you need some way of organizing all the things you see, that is, you need a rough mental blueprint. Such a blueprint is always based on *assumptions* about the limits and boundaries of human behavior.

Much interest used to be shown in assumptions about Basic Human Nature and about what, if anything, the political system could do about it. Scholars used to argue about questions such as whether man is basically greedy, sinful, a herd animal, capable of continual perfections, either aristocratic *or* slavish from birth, and so on. To some extent these arguments were useful because they called attention to the differences between things that are *conventional* (i.e., invented by humans and therefore changeable) and things that are *natural* (i.e., produced spontaneously and unintentionally as part of the biological cycle and therefore traditionally harder to change). The more science tells men about how to get what they want and the more clearly they are able to think about what it is they really want, the less useful these old-fashioned disputes prove to be. The question is no longer so much whether something results from physiological or psychological causes or whether certain people are ambitious because of their "natures" or because of the way they were brought up. The question *now* is: Can a process be changed? And if so, why and how?

For any *complete* theory of human behavior, it would be necessary to have a large number of assumptions (axioms), taken from philosophy, history, and the social sciences. Our present task is not to present an elaborate system of axioms, but to set out a *minimum* number of assumptions for the outline of a political system. These assumptions sound reasonable or self-evident at our present state of knowledge.

Assumption 1: Goals. All human behavior has goals (aims, objects, wants, opinions, meanings)—such as getting something done, making something happen, avoiding something, or hoping something will not happen. The goals are described in terms like happiness, self-fulfillment, survival, health, success, victory, and virtue. For this reason, people naturally inquire into what different behaviors mean, and they are not satisfied until they think they know (i.e., have some theory about) what they mean. During each person's lifetime, some of his goals get achieved, some are forgotten, and some prove to be impossible.

Assumption 2: Symbolism. Some things remind people of other things, or one thing is used as a short-hand for several things because a person believes the things to be connected, or because they make sense to him that way, or just because it is easier to remember them that way. This can lead to lots of confusion if people think they are talking the same language but in fact are only using similar-sounding words. (Someone in England recently claimed that Lady Godiva, protesting the harshness of her husband's government, rode through Coventry stripped, *not of her clothes,* but of her power and arrogance.) On the other hand, it can be very efficient because, like any other code, more meanings can be communicated in the same amount of time and space. The meanings (referents) of everyday life are highly concentrated and often vague.

Assumption 3: Individuality.   People may have different wants. This means that *different* people have different wants. It also means that the *same* person has different wants. It means further that the same person can have different wants of different intensities, i.e., that he can want both A and B, and at the same time prefer A to B. It also means that a person's wants can change: now more than anything he may want to travel, though last week more than anything he wanted to write a song.

Assumption 4: Sociability.   People often exhibit the same or similar wants. In some cases, this is because they just happen to be alike.   In other cases it is because they are imitating one another. In still other cases, it is because they are obeying the same authority who told them to behave the same way.

Assumption 5: Comparability.   For certain purposes it is useful to assume that people can be compared. For example, all 435 members of the U.S. House of Representatives are public officials. It *could* be that they have nothing else in common in the world; or it *could* be that they are identical in every other respect, too.

Assumption 6: Affirmation (Values).   Whether they know it or not, people by their choices and behaviors vote for what they think is worthwhile in life and against what they think is not. These affirmations of worth can be measured by what is given up. They cost something in terms of lost opportunities, time spent, money spent, degrees of interest, effort exerted, and so on. Since such affirmations cost something, they are investments; as investments they are defended against devaluation and loss. Hence, they are sources of fights and defensive measures. People find it hard to change their affirmations—it is painful for a person to admit he was wrong, or to accept what he was used to rejecting, or to leave the old homestead. (Las Vegas and other gambling operations are based on this reluctance to stop when you are losing. So are many wars.)

Assumption 7: Discontinuity.   People tend to assume that the objects they talk about are related. *Whether* they are connected is, of course, a question to be answered by going out and looking. Some things are most certainly connected; others are indirectly connected; and some are not connected at all. For example, a wage-earner who hides all his money in an old tin can is only weakly connected to the consumer-spending side of the economic system. Social scientists generally assume *both* (a) that all aspects of human behavior are related and (b) that they *may* be unrelated. The evidence determines which assumption is valid.

Assumption 8: Human Energy.   Under the best conditions imaginable, each person has only a limited amount of energy. After a while everyone gets fatigued, sleepy, careless, irritable, or silly. In our day-to-day lives, there is certainly a lot of wasted energy; but that is hard to avoid, and there remains only so much energy to do the serious work of society. Therefore, political systems have only a limited amount of energy at their disposal; even when a substantial attempt is made to get (or force) people to lend their energies to the political system, the available amount of energy is still limited. Since each political decision requires energy to make and more energy to carry it through to completion, the number of decisions that can be made and carried out in a political system depends on the number of people in it and on what part of their energies they will lend it.

Problem

1. Re-read this chapter after you complete Chapter 8; change some of the assumptions; and discuss how your new set of assumptions will change your picture of the political system.

Suggested Readings

Stuart Chase, *The Proper Study of Mankind* (1956).
John Dewey, *Logic, The Theory of Inquiry* (1938).
Lawrence Frank, *Nature and Human Nature* (1951).
Abraham Kaplan, *The Conduct of Inquiry* (1964).
Robert S. Lynd, *Knowledge for What?* (1939).
Donald MacIntosh, *Foundations of Human Society* (1969).
Rene Spitz, *No and Yes* (1957).

CHAPTER 2

Political Systems

A. SYSTEMS IN GENERAL

A SET is a number of things taken together for any reason. For example, all whole numbers (0, 1, 2, 3, . . . N) can be taken together as a set—the set of all whole numbers. The people on a particular city block at any given time can be considered a set. For things to belong to a set, it does not matter *what* connection there is between them, and it does not matter *whether* there is actually any connection between them.

If, however, the things in a set are related to one another in some special way, the result is a SYSTEM. A system is a set of things related in some way, so that changing or removing any one thing in the set will make a difference to other things in the system. Pneumonia, for instance, makes a difference to the whole physiological system. Doubling the number of people in a city would undoubtedly change the city in many ways.

The simplest system consists of two opposing elements (e.g., tall-short, in-out, present-absent, yes-no, peace-war). Since the elements are opposites, it is logically impossible to belong to the system without being part of one and only one element of this "binary opposition." That is to say, the *relation* between the two elements is not itself a *third* element in the system, as it would be if the elements "fitted together" or overlapped. For instance, in a system that had categories only for voters and non-voters in the election of a Pope, there would be no way of taking account fully of responses like "voted but wishes he hadn't" or "didn't vote though all his fellow Cardinals from Africa did."

Systems with human beings as the parts (or units) are generally known as SOCIAL SYSTEMS. One kind of social system is a *political system*.

B. POLITICAL SYSTEMS

The relation between people in a political system is called AUTHORITY. Authority exists when some people are willing to do what other people want. Thus, a POLITICAL SYSTEM is a system in which some people can get other people to do things that they would not want to do otherwise. Paying taxes and waiting for stop-lights are political acts. So are being drafted into the Army, being registered to vote, and being punished for coming to school or work late. So is being shot for treason.

There are people who are so simple-minded or nervous about politics that they want to reduce all of politics to a binary system—such as Communists vs. others, Catholics versus Protestants, The People versus The Interests, Aryans versus dark-skinned people.

People who have authority are usually known to other people by some title or position, such as leader, official, chief, boss, judge, parent, Senator, and so on. People give one another many reasons for using authority and for obeying authority. These reasons are called *political philosophies* or *ideologies*. It makes a lot of difference which ideology is used to explain the use of authority, because different ideologies give different rules for what should be done, when, and by whom. Most people try to reduce the number of things they have to do to satisfy the authorities. Therefore, most people have strong feelings about which ideology is best.

Everybody, during the course of his life, exercises authority, obeys authority, and disobeys authority. People tend to view those who are successful in exercising authority (i.e., leaders) as possessing some kind of magic. One reason for this view is that some people feel helpless in the modern world and count on the leaders to save them from trouble and to make their wishes come true. Another reason is that those who are unsuccessful at getting authority will tend to believe that there is something special, unusual, or unfair about those who *are* successful. Of course, many leaders have years of experience in the political system and have learned skills which increase their chances of winning.

For most people, it is very important to believe that what they want from the political system is *right*. If, for example, everybody could do anything and take *anything,* there would be no rules for satisfying some people's wants and not satisfying others. As long as there is not enough of everything to go around, people are going to be afraid of being left out. If they believe that their wants are *right,* and can convince other people, then they won't get left out.

Every time authority is exercised, somebody gets left out or gets less than he wanted of something. A political system has to develop in such a way that those who get left out still have hope that they may win out in the future—otherwise the losers may eventually get together and do something to change the political system.

A Crisis in a political system is the point at which it looks as if it is no longer going to be true that change in a part of the system will result in some change in the rest of the system. This can happen either because the system has internal troubles or is being changed by something outside itself. There are numerous reasons why crises develop (see Chapters 4 and 6).

A political crisis that begins *within* the system is called civil war, insurrection, subversion, rebellion, or revolution. One that begins *outside* the system is called invasion, attack, provocation, or imperialism. Many political disputes stem from disagreement over whether it is reasonable to believe that a crisis exists yet.

Some political systems exist across several countries: for example, tribes, like those who graze across the borders of Somalia and Ethiopia; peoples who live in more than one country, like the Armenians and Assyrians; and countries, like Cambodia or Canada, that contain different nationalities.

Another example of a political system is found in the relations between and among nations. We know that as far back as history goes countries had dealings with one another. Most often, these dealings were economic trading or war. Nowadays the relations among countries are very complicated. (Consider simply the airlines, or shipping patterns on the Great Lakes.) We shall refer to them as the INTERNATIONAL POLITICAL SYSTEM (IPS). It is like any other political system and can be understood with the concepts set forth in this book.

Since the international political system is not as tight (or well-integrated) as some political systems, the ways it fits together are less obvious. Its laws are called *treaties;* but they do not always apply to the whole system. Some of its laws are *customs,* or long-standing practices, and are hard to identify in abstract terms. The officials of the United Nations are leaders of the international political system, and so, clearly, are the leaders of the so-called super-powers (Russia, the United States, and perhaps China). "World public opinion" and "international prestige" are vague concepts, owing to the loose and broken-up quality of the IPS. What a particular country wants out of the IPS is known as that country's FOREIGN POLICY. Some people say that there isn't any IPS—that all there is is a big collection of all the foreign policies of the separate countries of the world. At the same time, it is possible to say that there *are not any separate countries,* that all there is is the IPS, which permits certain parts of the world to be run by the people who happen to live there. This second viewpoint may sound strange to you; but it is obviously possible for any one political system to be put out of business by the others, either through invasion, subversion, or, in some cases, boycott.

C. PARTIAL THEORIES

Equilibrium and Change

Nothing can so agitate social scientists as a discussion of social *change* and social *equilibrium* or *stability.* Since both change and stability are all around, one would think that both are problems we should try to understand. What often happens, however, is that social scientists who study change attack those who study stability as having a conservative bias (the real, and illogical, bias here is the assumption that people necessarily like whatever they study—an absurdity). The contrary is also true: people who study change are accused of having no respect for tradition and the social fabric.

Actually, of course, both questions must be answered. *How is it possible for political systems to last for a long time?* On the other hand, *how is it that all political systems invariably change* to a greater or lesser degree? The Incas of Peru established a society that was stable for a long time. Some of the reasons for this were the land tenure system (land was re-allocated every year so that everybody had about the same amount, thus preserving the relations among all individuals), the idea that the Inca was a deity and could not be challenged, and the fact that society took care of the dispossessed (thus preventing the development of frustrations that might have changed the system). But the Incan civilization changed (collapsed) with the Spanish conquest. Why it collapsed is not entirely clear, although there are many theories. What *is* clear is that the society was not able to deal with a new kind of external threat, even one that might have seemed to be much weaker than the Incas, who had a population of 11–12 million and a well-organized administration.

When dealing with social equilibrium, it is not meant that nothing is going on in a society. People may be doing things at a hectic and feverish pace. It is simply that they do the same things over and over again so that the elements in the system (e.g., wants, classes, groups, personalities) retain their usual relationships. If a person wanted to, he could establish different *kinds* of equilibrium states. One kind might be when *nothing* changes; another when a little change occurs but the other elements fight it off and *restore* the previous equilibrium (in the way white corpuscles destroy invading microbes so that a sick person begins to feel like his old self); and another when change occurs that very *gradually* changes the system but does not destroy its integrity (as, for example, the way puberty changes people but not so much that we can't still recognize them).

By the same token, when talking about social change, it is

not meant that the change has to be as extraordinary as the Incan collapse. That particular change was *intense* (it drastically affected the old system), *rapid* (the old system went under very quickly), and *broad* (just about everybody from the Inca on down was changed). Change can also be *moderate, slow,* and *selective.* In the Roman Empire, change occurred gradually over a long period, perhaps from the first century A.D. to the disintegration in the fifth century. Otto the Great was so far out of touch with reality that he believed himself to be the successor to the imperial Caesars as late as the tenth century! This proves that some people never get the message about how things have changed.

In the real world, people react to change and stability in different ways. For example, some people see that change is happening and do not like it (e.g., the Tories didn't like it when Labor won in Britain after World War II and they expected all sorts of dire things to happen). Others *deny* that change is occurring when it really is (e.g., some say that the Negroes in American really were content in the 50s and 60s, but got steamed up only by a bunch of opportunistic agitators). Also, some people see change of a sort that really isn't happening (e.g., the Bolsheviks thought, wrongly, that the German workers would make a Communist revolution soon after 1917). Still others see that things are highly stable and are dissatisfied (e.g., the "hippies" would like to see some changes in society, but many apparently do not think it is very likely). In short, you can tell a great deal about a person's politics and personality if you know whether he likes change or stability and what *sorts* of change he prefers, if any (see Chapter 4).

What has to be kept in mind, of course, is that what people *think* about change and stability is not always very helpful (see Chapter 6) in telling us whether things *really are* stable or changing. That is a scientific question which we have to investigate very carefully, keeping our preferences out of it. Some scientists say stability is produced by socialization (teaching people to like the current system) and by social control (punishing or getting rid of people who have not been socialized "adequately"). There are many theories of change, most of them useful, but all of them inadequate. Some say man's natural curiosity produces change; others that invention and innovation caused by necessity and wars cause change; still others that new family patterns (with their new authority structures) are really the sources of change; and still others say that unstable personalities and crack-pots can get a lot of change going. Some sources of change are clear, as when the West invaded Asia and Africa in colonial days.

There are various theories about which aspects or combinations of change and stability are most important for understanding the political system. We shall refer to these as "partial theories" because they do not pretend to account for all the goings-on within the political system. The following are examples of partial theories, all of which apply to other sectors of human social behavior and not just to political life.

Game Theory

Some people think that politics resembles a game or can best be understood if thought of as a kind of game. We have all heard people refer to "the great game of politics" or "the game of life"; and people say (in exasperation), "I'm not going to play this game."

Politics does have much in common with conventional games: it has players (people), rules (constitutions, laws, and other agreements), objectives (like seizing or winning the White House, rather than the opponent's bishop or queen in a chess game), and excitement. The simplest political game to understand is one between two players who both want the same prize and either (a) refuse to share it or (b) believe it to be the sort of prize that cannot be divided. Since in this game the loser gets "zero" and the winner takes all, it is known as a "zero-sum game." (The winnings minus the losings equal zero.) In politics there are many examples of this game. Lyndon Johnson won all of the Presidency in 1964, and Barry Goldwater didn't get any of it. Members of Parliament in England engage in a zero-sum game because only one player at a time can win in each district. Zero-sum games are games of *pure conflict,* which means not that the players are necessarily angry with one another, but that by co-operating neither can get what he wants.

There are also games of *pure cooperation.* The United States and the Soviet Union are both interested (sometimes) in avoiding a third world war. Therefore, both countries want to avoid any sort of competition that would start World War III and to engage in any form of cooperation that will steer clear of such competition.

Games against nature can be games of pure cooperation because nature is indifferent to the outcome. That is, nature does not play the game with the same kind of deliberation as a human player. Hence, people can work together to defeat polio, rabies, and malaria; or they can work together to grow more food for everyone or to predict bad weather.

Most political games, however, are neither cases of pure conflict nor of pure cooperation. They are "mixed-motive" games or simply *mixed games*. In this sort of game, a person may not be sure to what extent he wants to cooperate with others and to what extent he wants to fight with them. A famous example is Prisoners' Dilemma. It is really a very interesting puzzle, and you might want to try to solve it:

Two people are arrested together and charged with committing a crime as accomplices. They are kept in separate cells. They are told that if both confess to the crime, each will probably get 5 years in prison. If neither confesses, both will probably get 3 years in prison. If one confesses and the other remains silent, the one who confesses will go free and the other will probably get 8 years in prison. What would you do if you were one of the prisoners?

There are also more complicated kinds of political games—games in which many people are involved, so-called non-zero-sum games, and ones in which people can change sides or form coalitions. There is still a lot to learn about the ways in which the political system resembles games and why different people have learned and accepted different rules of the game.

The world takes the shape of the game.

Exchange Theory

Another way of analyzing human behavior, including politics, is called exchange theory. It is quite simple, as are all good theories. The basic idea is contained in familiar sayings, such as,

"You can't get something for nothing," "Everything has its price," and "If you want to dance, you've got to pay the fiddler." In politics, the things people pay for are *public policies,* which is to say, highways, schools, social welfare programs, weapons, wars, and sometimes peace.

In democratic countries, there is supposed to be a very efficient way for the people to enter into an exchange with the politicians: people give *support* to the politicians (by voting for them, paying their taxes, obeying the draft laws, and so on), and the politicians in return are supposed to do what the people want.

Politics is just one of the *arenas* or *markets* in which exchanges go on in a society. In the political arena, too, each party has to take on certain *costs* in return for the *benefits* received. Thus, the people may have to pay higher taxes for the highways which some politicians are offering to "sell" them. To "buy" the highways from these politicians means to forgo the possibility of buying some of the things that other politicians are offering to sell the voters.

We may assume that the people can't buy all the policies being offered, because all policies cost *something,* and people have a limited number of things to give in exchange for policies. The politicians also have costs. They have to run for office, seek campaign contributions, suffer the slings and arrows of their opponents, make speeches, and spend less time with their families than they might like. On the other hand, they get many of the things that some people want very badly—things like power, deference, fame, and so forth.

People can thus be viewed as trying to get more than they have, subject to what they have to give up to get it. This is true of all political participants. When it is to the mutual advantage of people in politics, they will exchange costs and benefits. As a consequence, everyone will be better off than he was before the exchange. When a person has used his resources in the best way he can, then the political system is said to be *in equilibrium.* This simply means here that no one has any reason to exchange costs and benefits with anyone else for the time being. In reality, of course, the resources of people continually change, or they find out (by getting more information) that they have not been getting all they could. Even getting information is a change in resources. So what might be said is that there is a *tendency* for the political system to move toward an equilibrium, but that new things always prevent its attainment.

Moreover, the fact is that resources are not equitably distributed in society. Some people obviously have more than others. Those who have more may make greater or fancier demands on the politicians, and will get more in return for their contributions, than will the people with measly resources.

One of the things exchange theory tries to explain is why *particular* people enter the political system at all and why they enter it at the *point or part* they do. In 1954, the National Association for the Advancement of Colored People encouraged Negro parents to enter the judicial part of the political system and to get a favorable public policy (desegregation) from the policy-makers. In the early 1940s, Jehovah's Witnesses also entered the U.S. judicial system, in this case to be relieved of the requirement of saluting the flag in school ceremonies. (They believed that God alone should command their loyalty.) On the other hand, some people—lobbyists—concentrate their political efforts on particular legislative committees, while still other people enter political arenas by trying to influence the Prime Minister, the Parliament, provincial leaders and legislators, or public opinion generally. The American Medical Association, for instance, entered *all* these arenas in fighting President Truman's public health insurance bill in 1948.

One reason for entering different parts of the political system is that, although similar policies may be made in the different arenas, it is cheaper to get what you want in this or that arena. Many units of government make tax policy, and if someone wants lower taxes he can work on different sets of politicians. However, it may be easier in the case of lower taxes to try to get them at the grass roots—from Calgary rather than from Ottawa. If you want to change foreign policy, however, there are not so many arenas to choose from.

What a person has to decide, then, is where he can get what he wants, how much it will cost at alternative places, and how much he can get with his limited resources and other wants. When these questions are answered, it will then be known (1) which political arenas a person will enter, (2) what policies he will demand there, and (3) how much of those policies he will demand.

As a result of the answers to these questions, a few people end up by entering politics at many places, some people enter politics only to vote, and large numbers of people decide not to enter politics at all—they think even the cost of voting is too high in terms of any good it will do them.

Structural-Functional Analysis

One of the most popular, and also most criticized, ways in which social and political things can be examined is through structural-functional analysis, sometimes called just "functionalism." The ideas basic to this approach are easy to grasp, although the problems with the method raise very difficult questions.

Essentially, this approach first directs attention to the social structures, or institutions, which are in some way involved in the problems that interest the analyst. Used in this sense, institutions are not simply formal organizations, such as Congress, the Federal Bureau of Investigation, or Rotary International, but also families, political machines, electoral systems, crime syndicates, bookmaking, and political demonstrations. A social structure is defined by the *interactions* of people. If two or more people interact periodically for any reason, and if their roles— what each person actually *does* in the interaction—are reasonably stable, then a social structure or institution is said to exist.

It is thus important to be able to identify the persistent relationship that makes up the proposed structure. If a change in one of the relationships does *not* affect the others, this relationship is not a structural element. If two ships pass in the dark, removal of one ship will not affect the behavior of the other: hence their relationship is not a functional one nor does it constitute an interaction. Passengers on a train do not comprise a social institution if they do not know one another and ride the train only infrequently. Passengers on a commuter train, however, who play bridge, reserve seats for their friends, and commiserate together over the deplorable incompetence of the transit authority, do comprise a social structure.

Thus, many social structures exist, whether obvious or not. The question, however, is this: what are the *consequences* of the relationships that obtain in the social structure in terms of their own survival and the survival of other structures. When a relationship enhances the structure's chances of survival, the relationship is regarded as *functional*. If the social structure's probability of survival is *reduced* by things that go on in an institution, those things are *dysfunctional*. Of course, what goes on in a structure may have little or no impact on its survival, in which case it is probably not very interesting scientifically. (Try to think of relationships that are neither functional nor dysfunctional in this sense. Hard to do, isn't it?) Cigarette smoking, by all scientific accounts, is dysfunctional to the person as an organism and may lead to an early death. Appropriate servings of salt, calcium, and vitamin C, on the other hand, are required for good health and are thus functional to the survival of the person.

We must also point out that the same activity may be both functional *and* dysfunctional, depending on its consequences for different social structures. A political demagogue who indulges in inflammatory speechmaking may assist his political party in winning elections but may also divide the society as a whole, provoking widespread confusion, disarray, harsh recriminations, and perhaps collapse of the community.

The objective (actual) consequences of any social structure are often quite well-known. Everybody knows that the U.S. Congress passes laws, that the federal system of government in Canada provides a measure of local autonomy, and that police departments capture criminals. These well-known functions of various structures are called *manifest functions*.

Not all functions of social structures are immediately obvious, however. These less obvious functions are referred to as *latent functions*. It is a little bit like detective work to discover them. In fact, the good social scientist is often the one who can discover more latent functions of a structure than anyone else.

A school system, for example, not only performs the manifest function of educating children, but also has consequences, such as giving jobs to the superintendent of schools, to teachers, and to specialists in budgeting, purchasing, personnel, and contracting. Since the school system needs land and buildings, real estate men, building contractors, labor unions, and architects will also be affected by it. If school attendance is compulsory, people will be in school who otherwise would be out competing for jobs, working in the family business, helping around the house, roaming the streets, practicing the guitar, or whatever.

These latent functions become obvious when we think about them. A less obvious function is that the school may become a source of pride for the community if its building is particularly big or impressive or if its basketball team wins the state championship. In these cases, the function of the school would be to integrate the neighborhood or the town by producing a sense of solidarity in the community. In another case, the successful basketball coach or the dynamic principal may use the school to advance his career by employing his success in one system to move to another job with higher salary, greater prestige, more power, or better basketball players. The school may also be very important to certain parents because they view education as the best way for their children to obtain a reasonable standard of living or to learn a cultivated style of life. Another latent function of the school might be to prove that everybody is alike and, thus, to discourage learning and individuality.

One problem in seeking latent functions is the tendency of some people to find very insidious functions which are not quite clear to other observers. The Paul Revere Association, Yeomen, Inc., for example, has said that a latent function of the nuclear test ban treaty is that we will all end up with "the Russians and Zionists ruling the world, all Christianity wiped out, and all wives, mothers, and daughters in the brothels of Asia, China, and India."

You may want to know what criticisms can be made concerning structural-functionalism. One danger is that many of its advocates seem to impute a teleology (=being directed toward an end or shaped by a purpose) to all social structures. Scientifically, this is a fallacy because we cannot simply assume that social structures exist *because* of the beneficial functions they are alleged to perform. (Benjamin Franklin once committed this fallacy in jest, when he said that Providence intended men to drink, else why should one's elbow function so nicely in raising cup to lip?)

Even if a given structure does do what we think is appropriate, we should not necessarily assume that some other structure could not do the job better. If Parent-Teacher Associations were disbanded, perhaps we could devise an even better structure to improve the schools.

There is also the tendency of functionalists to look only at the benefits produced by particular structures and not to subtract the costs from the benefits to get a more accurate picture of the structure. Or, when costs *are* subtracted and the benefits still predominate, there is a tendency then to say that the structure is socially useful and, at least by implication, should be preserved. But this, you can see, does not necessarily follow since still other structures may yield greater benefits and even lower costs.

The core of structural-functionalism is in the effort to identify structures, functions, and dysfunctions, but if we were to simply *list* the functions and dysfunctions of any structure we might conclude that structural-functionalism is rather banal scientifically. If this were the case no "if-then" kind of statements or real propositions would have been developed; nor would we have produced any real scientific *theory.* Used in this way structural-functionalism reduces to a parody of what social science should be doing.

Actually, structural-functionalism, used imaginatively and with a flair, is very valuable in generating insights and ideas susceptible to scientific analysis. If we were to reduce *The Trojan Women* or *The Adventures of Huckleberry Finn* to propositional form, they too would appear banal and simplistic. But viewed as wholes they are revealing analyses of intriguing problems and relationships. This too may be the virtue of good functional social analysis. In the hands of such as Robert Merton or Talcott Parsons, functionalism may increase our knowledge of the world. Functionalism is more concerned, then, with substance than with scientific method.

Finally, we must observe that functionalism is quite useful in *comparative* political analysis. It reminds us that some structures look alike and do similar things; some things look alike and do very *dis*similar things; and some *look* different but do quite the same things. Both the U.S. Congress and the Indian Parliament appear to be major policy-making bodies; the Congress, however, makes more policy than the Parliament, which usually "rubber-stamps" decisions made by the leading political party or coalition. You can see how confusing it is to compare structures—you might not be comparing things that are at all similar. One way of getting around this, therefore, is to compare functions.

Classes

Another partial theory of society and politics is one that emphasizes *social classes*. A social class is ordinarily much larger than a group, an elite, or, by definition, any individual. Class is, therefore, a very large variable, or unit of analysis, in the understanding of politics. The only larger variable might be the nation-state which is often the basic unit in the international political system.

A class is made up of individuals who (1) get together on a basis of equality, (2) have many of the same ideas and who act somewhat alike, and (3) are set apart from the rest of society by social beliefs about inferiority and superiority. These criteria can be made as refined as one might want, but three or four major classes are usually discussed: the upper class, the middle class, and the lower, or perhaps working, class. An important thing to remember is that classes are not completely static; there is always some movement from one class to another. That movement is not always *upward* (as when a tenant-farmer's son becomes Secretary of State). It may also be *downward* (as when the French aristocracy was put out of business) or *lateral* (as when a doctor's son becomes a lawyer). These movements are important because they have a lot to do with political changes. A *caste* system, on the other hand, is a system in which no mobility of any importance can occur between castes (although it is possible within a caste).

Classes have been viewed in two major ways by value theorists. Some people favor a class system in which the classes have different amounts of power, deference, and income. These people often say that mankind is naturally divided into classes on the basis of talent, wisdom, or morality so that it would be unnatural to want to eliminate classes. Others do want to eliminate classes since they believe that the overclass always exploits the underclass.

Scientifically, one would want to know how classes affect social consensus and social conflict. Marx believed that mankind would go on fighting until classes were eliminated because various classes had different interests that could not be reconciled by any amount of good-will, bargaining, or compromise. Others say that things are not that bad—that if all people can improve themselves, or if their children can, then nobody will want to fight anybody else. What do you think?

Moral Theory

One way of looking at the political system (and it used to be the chief way of studying political science) is to ask: What are the most important principles of political action? This is a partial theory because it emphasizes a particular value or set of values, to the neglect of other aspects of political reality. It is moral or ethical because it is more interested in showing people what they ought to be doing than in showing them how the political system as a whole works. This kind of theory usually promotes particular values—justice, virtue, self-interest, power, consensus, The Nation, racism—and explores the implications of these values for the political system and for other values. Since the purpose is to excite people to say the right things and to feel certain conventional emotions and abandon others, it is perhaps more accurate to refer to this approach as indoctrination rather than as theory. At all events, it is easy to see that the moralists' approach to the political system does not add much to scientific understanding, for the energy that would have been spent examining the system has to be used condemning or cheering it. Everyone possesses these enthusiasms, however, and it would be dishonest to pretend that there exist any theories of human behavior which do not contain *some* little element of moral theory.

Theories of this type are the proper subject-matter of political philosophy, and it is not necessary to discuss them here, except for one example. The example of pluralist and elitist theories is useful both because it will show how moral and scientific elements can become fused in a single theory and also because it is now being used to explain things about political systems all over the world.

Pluralist and Elite Theories

Many attempts have been made to explain politics in terms of *who* has power. Some people, for example, argue that power in the United States is widely scattered and is to be found in various sorts of groups. These people tend to say that individuals do not have much or any power, but that if they want to get some, they can join a group.

Some of these theories say that different groups have different amounts of power, but that every group has at least a little power and that groups are the most significant elements in the political picture. Common-sense examples would be the AFL–CIO, the American Legion, the National Education Association, and the Mafia. Groups are said to have different wants or interests (although they really do not, since only individual human beings can have wants). And when groups want the same thing, the result is either conflict or compromise or alliance-building. Those groups with the most power will win the most of what the groups are fighting over. Power is supposed to be defined by such things as the number of people in the group, their social standing, their social and political skills, the quality of leadership in the group, the degree of access of politicians, money, and whether or not the goals are close to the basic myths of the society. People who believe these sorts of propositions are said to have a *pluralist* or group theory of politics.

A good question is: If all of these groups are in conflict, why do they not end up in such a donnybrook that nothing is left of the society? A frequent answer is: This does not happen because of *overlapping memberships*. That is, if one person belongs to two or more groups, then the conflict between or among the groups will be reduced because all groups are afraid of driving out those people who may also belong to other groups. Thus, it is said that groups temper, or limit, the demands that they make upon other groups in the society. Another reason that is sometimes given is that the "rules of the game" keep conflict within limits. For instance, all (or most) groups would rather lose a fight with another group than resort to violence in the hope of winning. There are other rules, presumably, that also limit fights between groups.

The trouble with the pluralist theory is that: (1) most Americans do not even belong to interest groups; (2) overlapping memberships, to the extent that they exist at all, probably reinforce conflict rather than limit it, since people tend to belong to groups with the same general ideologies rather than to groups with conflicting ideologies; (3) it is not possible to predict anything from the theory; and (4) it does not explain how the rules of the game came about or what they are. (After all, if all policy is the product of group conflict, then the rules of the game had to be formed by group conflict; but if there were no rules in the first place, then why did some groups limit their conduct with respect to the non-existent rules?) Actually, group theory has been used to increase the knowledge of politics; but that is because it called attention to the role of association in the political process (see Chapter 8).

Another difficulty with pluralist theory is that it often assumes that it is a *good thing* to have many different interests in a society competing and compromising. It is assumed, moreover, that the interactions of these groups lead (somehow) to a more stable political system and to a more varied, richer society. We have just suggested that the argument can be turned around and that it can be assumed just as freely that the exercise of power by numerous competing groups can lead to chaos and instability. As to the moral ingredient in the theory, it can be seen without much reflection that it is a good thing to have such political variety in a society if and only if the criteria of "good" happen to agree with the *outcome* of such a political process. Some people think it is good to tolerate many different approaches to life and decision-making; other people find it shamefully inefficient and degenerate.

A rather different view of who has power is provided by elite theory.[1] There are many theories about elites, but one of the best-known versions (referring to American society) claims that authentic power is in the hands of a very few people who occupy leading positions in the military, in the corporations, and in the executive branch of government. There are some people who have moderate amounts of power, but, say the supporters of this theory, they actually have much less than they themselves and the social scientists think they have.

This illusion of power is said to be caused by the fact that: (1) those people who have a little power like to think that they are very powerful; (2) social scientists have access to only the middle-levels of power, and so that is all they write about; and (3) the groups with real power—the power elite—will not admit that they have as much power as they do, so that just about everybody ends up being confused. Those in the middle level of power play politics in about the way the pluralists describe; this level includes structures like the Supreme Court, the Congress, labor unions, governors of states, interest groups, churches, Yale University, and so on. Those people who believe in the power elite agree with the pluralists that individuals do not have any power, but they go further and say that, since most people are not members of either the power elite or the middle levels of power, most people have no power at all.

If this is true, then why don't the people rise up and throw the rascals out? This is always a good question to ask of any theory; that is, what keeps the system going? The supporters of the power elite theory say that there are two things: they say it is fear, on the one hand (if people get too far out of line with what the elite wants, they will be punished), and manipulation of the mass media on the other (if people are given only a few of the real facts, then they will have no basis upon which to question any public decisions).

There are problems with this theory, as with all theories. It is probably true that people can actually get more information about what is going on than the power elite theorists are willing

[1] Since elites exist in all classes and castes, elite theory is somewhat different from class theory.

to admit. And it is probably true that most people obey the government not directly because of fear, but because of the belief that they *should* obey the government (see *Socialization* in Chapter 6). Furthermore, one can point to many important decisions (e.g., the desegregation decisions reached by the U.S. Supreme Court) that evidently have not been made by any members of the so-called power elite.

An earlier version of elite theory (still a popular item on the academic menu) said that individuals vary a good deal in their talents and that the more intelligent souls or the ones with special political talents *ought* to be running the government. This theory is plainly relevant to the problems of democratic theory. It involves, among other things, an (unnecessary) ambiguity: in any known society there are always some people (elites) who have powers or skills that others do not have; so the question of who these people are has to be distinguished from the question of whether they are basically (by nature) better at certain things than the others. And both those questions have to be distinguished from the question: Is it, according to specifiable criteria, a *good thing* to have a political system in which the decisions are made by this or that elite? By confounding these questions, the elite theory has sometimes made it impossible to answer any of them. No one can deny that Denmark has a King. The answer to the question, "Does Denmark have a King?" is "Yes." That's easy. It is not so easy to say which of all the other people who live in Denmark would make as good or better a King as the present one. It is still harder to say whether it is a good idea to have *any* King.

Sample Theorem

No one can have no effect on a political system.

Proof A

(i) There is no system such that some element is not proximately or remotely connected with all other parts of the system (*Ex def.* System).

(ii) The elements of a political system are the wants of the people in the system (*Ex def.* Political System).

(iii) All people have wants; all wants belong to people; and only people can make authoritative decisions about wants (Assumptions 1, 3, 4, and 6).[2]

(iv) Therefore, by definition, a person having no wants and making no decisions about wants could not exist nor affect the political system. And conversely, any person who exists, has wants, and makes decisions about them can affect the political system.

Proof B

(i) A political system exists if and only if authoritative decisions need to be made (*Ex def.* Political system).

(ii) Decisions need to be made only if there are conflicts (*Ex def.* Conflict and Decision; Chapters 3 and 4).

(iii) Conflicts result from inconsistent wants (*Ex def.* Conflict).

(iv) All people have wants (Assumptions 1, 3, and 6).

(v) Since wants either are or are not consistent and since any want may substitute for any other consistent want without affecting a conflict, any want *can* become an object of conflict and can thereby affect the political system.

(vi) Since any want can affect the political system, any person can; since any person can, there is no one who cannot.

Proof C

(i) All people have opinions (Assumptions 1, 3, and 6).

(ii) An authoritative decision cannot be made unless the wants of some person(s) are adopted by some other(s) (*Ex def.* Political System and Decision).

(iii) For the wants of the one person to be *adopted* by another, they must be known to the other.

---

[2] Assumptions are stated in Chapter 1.

(iv) To make known a want is to make known an opinion (*Ex def.* Opinion).

(v) To make known the acceptance or rejection of a decision is to make known an opinion (*Ex def.* Opinion).

(vi) The opinions of the decision-maker(s) affect the wants they make known (Assumption 6).

(vii) Anyone in a political system can be the *object* of a decision (*Ex def.* and Proof A), and anyone who can be the object of a decision can thereby make known an opinion (Step v).

(viii) Hence, there is no one who cannot affect a political system.

Sample Theorem.

Without coercion, there can be no political system.

Proof

(i) There is no political system without authority (*Ex def.*).

(ii) Authority is the adoption by B of one or more of A's wants (*Ex def.*).

(iii) If B *already* wants what A wants, there has been no exercise of authority (Implication).

(iv) Coercion is to be made to do something (*Ex def.*).

(v) Since there is no authority where no one can be made to do what he does not want to do, there can be a political system if and only if someone can prevent others from doing only what they want.

Problems

1. What would become of a political system if, as some philosophers have imagined, it worked so well that everyone in it either (a) did everything the authorities wanted him to do, to the letter of the law, or (b) was given *no* commands by the authorities?

2. In a country like the U.S.A., how does the death of a plumber, age 45, in good health previously, lacking any college education, affect the political system?

3. If the king used to collect taxes every other year, checking up on every tenth taxpayer, and now he collects taxes monthly and uses IBM computers to check up on *every* taxpayer, is the *political* system any different? If so, how?

4. Everyone will recall that the inventory of military equipment taken at Dover castle in 1343 by the Earl of Huntington, outgoing Warden of the Cinque Ports, and handed over to his successor, Sir Bartholomew Berghersh, showed the equipment to be in serious disrepair, even though Dover was a principal English fortress and England was at war with France in 1343. In terms of exchange theory, what might have been the cause of this seemingly deplorable state of affairs?

Suggested Readings

Mark Abrahamson, *The Professional in the Organization* (1967).
Aristotle, *Politics* (c. 329 B.C.).
James M. Buchanan and Gordon Tullock, *The Calculus of Consent* (1962).
Robert Curry and L. L. Wade, *A Theory of Political Exchange* (1968).
Anthony Downs, *An Economic Theory of Democracy* (1957).
David Easton, *The Political System* (1956).
David Easton, *A Systems Analysis of Political Life* (1965).
Albert Hirschman, *Journeys toward Progress* (1965).
James Madison, *Federalist #10* (1787).
Robert Merton, *Social Theory and Social Structure* (1957).
C. Wright Mills, *The Power Elite* (1956).
William C. Mitchell, *The American Polity* (1962).
Plato, *Republic* bks. vi–vii (c. 360 B.C.).
Lucian Pye, *Aspects of Political Development* (1966).
L. L. Wade and Robert Curry, *A Logic of Public Policy* (1970).
W. Lloyd Warner, *Social Class in America* (1949).
Mayer Zald, ed., *Social Welfare Institutions* (1965).

CHAPTER 3

Decisions

A DECISION is made when something is given up in favor of something else. The things may be physical objects, activities, opportunities, attitudes, or emotional needs such as the need for vengeance.

If something is not given up, what is happening is not a decision. It is often overlooked that *inaction* and the postponing of decisions are themselves decisions, *if* the chance to make certain kinds of decisions has been given up by delaying too long. Since political decisions almost always involve conflicts—because the decision-maker does not want to give up either alternative, though he knows he cannot really have it both ways—*kinds* of decisions and decision-making will also be discussed under the heading of Conflict-Resolution (see Chapter 5).

A decision should not be confused with a *routine,* nor should it be confused with a *preference.* A routine is a more or less fixed way of doing something, so that people can perform a task almost automatically, habitually, *without* making decisions about it. For example, the procedure for alerting the U.S. Strategic Air

Command required a certain number of steps, beginning with the President telling the Secretary of Defense or the SAC Generals to get the routine going. It is usually said that it is time to alternate from Step 1 to Step 2 in a routine, or to proceed from Step 2 to Step 3, and so on. This is because the steps have already been decided upon as the best way to do the job. *Deciding to use* a routine is a different matter and should not be confused with the routine itself.

Preferences are simply what you like and what you do not like and are comparisons between and among your likes and dislikes. Thus, preferences are both the *bases* of decision-making and the *effects* of decisions: if you prefer a new playground for River City instead of a public parking lot, you will probably vote for the candidates who promise to build the playground; and if enough other citizens vote like you, then the *outcome* is that River City will get the playground (i.e., a social preference has been demonstrated for the playground).

Problems arise in decision-making when: (1) a person is not sure what his own preferences are; (2) he is mistaken as to the likelihood that this or that preference can be attained in reality; (3) other people have conflicting preferences; or (4) he *believes* that they do. Uncertainty about preferences and real or imaginary disagreements over preferences lead to conflicts.

A CONFLICT is what happens when two things that cannot actually exist at the same time are wanted at the same time. In speaking of decisions, it can be said that a *decisional conflict* exists when a person wants to make a decision but does not want to do what needs to be done to make the decision.

Many political decisions are hard to make for the same reasons: because the people in a political system do not agree about what alternatives *actually are* available; because they do not agree about which are the *acceptable* alternatives; and because they are not sure about *their own preferences* in some cases.

A POLITICAL DECISION is, therefore, a decision where (1) some people are prevented from getting what they want *and* (2) some people end up willing to do what they did not want to do.

The number of topics on which rulers can made decisions without first consulting people is called the ruler's DECISION LATITUDE. The ruler has more decision latitude when: (1) his wants are the same as those of most other people in the political system; (2) he rules a system that will keep going without much consultation; (3) he already has very good information about what will and will not be accepted by the other people; or (4) he changes his wants so they *become* the same as other people's.

Methods for secretly increasing decision latitude in devious ways are known as *corruption*. Bribery, fraud, blackmail, and such, are ways of evading the decisions that bind other people and of devising new sorts of decisions.

Since there are usually people in the political system who cannot decide what they want and people who do not let anybody know what they want, political decisions are almost always made without knowing what some people truly want and what they will accept (see Chapter 7). When the decision-makers are badly misinformed about what the other people want and what they will accept, there can be much confusion, anger, unhappiness, crime, disrespect for authority, and loss of interest in politics. In some cases, this leads to revolution (civil war). The reason is that people usually *hope* they can work together to get what they want; and when it turns out that they cannot get along together or cannot get what they want when they *do* work together, they become disappointed and become despairing or feel that other people in the community are looking down on them.

Some people are so eager to get along with others that they will agree to all sorts of decisions just to keep from fighting. (It is also true that there are people who will go to great lengths to start fights and prevent decisions, once they are disappointed or bored with the political system.) This being so, it would be difficult in some political systems to make *any* decisions if it were not that people are, from childhood on, *used to* obeying the authorities and willing to punish themselves and others for refusing to obey.

Decisions that are made in politics (or anywhere, really) are of four general kinds. They include: (1) decisions which change old things in important ways or which start important new things going in a big way; and (2) decisions that add to, or subtract from, old things just a little bit or which start new things going in a small way. The first kind of decision could be called *comprehensive* and the second kind *incremental*. Also, decisions can be (3) coordinated and well-planned or (4) they can each be taken without paying any attention to the other decisions that are being made. Here the third type of decision is called *integrated* and the fourth type *fragmented*. If one looks at the possible combinations of these four kinds of decisions, the result is a *typology* like the one in Figure 1.

It is often claimed that decisions of the Type A pattern are most common within the United States. In other words, different people who do not work together very closely make many small decisions. If you think that life in the U.S. is rather predictable and highly specialized, with no one paying much attention to anyone else, maybe it is because you have been affected only by Type A kinds of decisions. So you hear people say, "Why doesn't someone do something," and "Nothing ever happens around here." Actually, a lot is happening, and many people are doing things. It is just that the pace, or speed, of decision-making sometimes makes it appear as if nothing much is changing.

A Type C decision pattern would be evidenced in such situations as in the Congo after independence or in France after the Revolution of 1789. Very big and important things happen, but many of them do not seem to make sense (i.e., they are difficult to understand) because they are not coordinated. Nobody knows who thought up the whole thing, if anybody. This kind of decision pattern can cause much hardship and insecurity; but, of course, so can the others.

In Communist countries, Type D decision patterns are sometimes found. Great plans are made and every aspect of the plans is arranged as carefully as possible. The "Great Leap Forward" in China was a Type D decision.

A Type B pattern might be found, say, in a country like

FIGURE 1. TYPES OF DECISIONS

	Fragmented	Integrated
Incremental	A	B
Comprehensive	C	D

Sweden or Britain. These are stable societies where radically new decisions are not often made (in fact, some tourists think that they are "boring" for that reason), but where the government tries to keep everything neat, tidy, and coordinated.

To say that these are the main kinds of decisions that get made in any given society is not to say (1) that other patterns are not sometimes found in the society or (2) that any particular decision will either succeed or fail. For example, the U.S. departed from Type A during World War II and started following Type D. This happened because most of the country decided that everybody had to get together and make some big plans to defeat Hitler and our other enemies. Also, it might be said that Type A decisions lead to the neglect of some problems, such as air and water pollution, because everyone cannot get together long enough to think through the whole problem. On the other hand, Type A decisions have given many Americans a very affluent way of life. In other words, it might be said that *if* people want to do something, say X, *then* they should select that decision pattern that will enable them to get what they want— otherwise they either will not get it or will have to pay more than they really have to.

However, there is another side to the story. What people *should* do and what they *can* do are quite different things. It may be that coordinated decisions cannot be made rationally because a person cannot hold all the information in his head long enough to integrate his decisions. Humans have limited capacities, but the problems may be virtually unlimited. Besides, someone may think that he has all the information necessary for a "good" decision, only to find out later that he really did not. Thus, he may get what he did not want and never intended to get. For example, a young man may *think* he knows how his bride-to-be is going to act, but the divorce statistics indicate that he may very well be wrong. Then, too, a person may not have the power to decide what he would really like to decide. All of these things mean that what people really do, or usually do, is this: they just muddle along trying to get by as best they can. There are, however, some techniques that are coming into use that may enable people to consider more facts and more consequences in their decisions. Two of these techniques are linear programming and operations research. They have not been used too much yet, but they may eventually improve the kinds of decisions that are made in the government.

More things usually go into a decision than you may realize. Even when your mind is perfectly clear about the factors that lead you to a decision, you may not want everybody else to know your reasons. And thus it is that you may find people guessing and disputing about what the decision-makers' "real" reasons were. (This is an exciting pastime, as you already know.)

To make a little picture of decision-making, you have to ignore all of these hidden and unintended factors. This is the *rational model* of decision-making—it assumes that you know what you want, why you want it, what realistic choices are available, and how a decision can be made (carried through). Please do not raise the objection that decisions are never so clear-cut! Everyone knows that already and cannot help it; what we are discussing here is a hypothetical decision in which skill and intelligence could be used to the utmost.

Thus, the model would look like this: you would first look at your own priorities $(P_1, P_2 \ldots P_n)$, or what you want to obtain by your behavior in the short run. Then you would scan the alternatives $(A_1, A_2 \ldots A_n)$ that exist in the surroundings. You would then compare the alternatives to your general criteria of choice $(C_1, C_2 \ldots C_n)$, that is, those conditions that are or are not so embarrassing to you as to be unacceptable. You then eliminate some quantity (x) of the alternatives because they clash with your general criteria. This leaves fewer alternatives $(A_n - x)$. You then compare the remaining alternatives with your present priorities, eliminating alternatives one by one as each is the worst remaining way of satisfying your priorities. The last remaining alternative is called the decision (A_d). Note that *all* the alternatives *could* be unacceptable, such that you decide the best alternative is to make *no* decision now. A simple diagram of the process is presented in Figure 2.

If you want to understand a specific decision (e.g., the decision to drop atomic bombs on Japan), a good way to proceed is to first break it down by identifying the individuals who participated in it. (One definition of power, incidentally, is participation in the making of decisions.) After locating the right individuals, you could then examine their *decisional premises,* or all the things that influence them. One could look, for example,

FIGURE 2. RATIONAL MODEL OF DECISION-MAKING

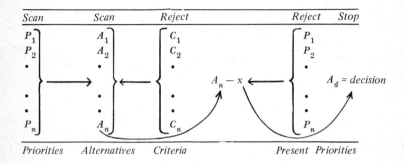

at their social-class background, their standing in associations, their ambitions, their ideologies, the factual information they had, and so forth. If you went far enough in this direction, chances are you would finally come to an explanation of the decision. By doing this, one might discover that what is *said* to be a cause of something, or the reason behind something, is not at all true. Thus, you cannot take for granted any explanation offered by the decision-maker himself; you have to go out and find out for yourself.

Sample Theorem

The fewer the decision-makers in a political system, the more decisions get made.

Proof

(i) Only a limited amount of human energy is available to any political system (Assumption 8).

(ii) A decision is the abandonment of one or more alternatives (*Ex def.*).

(iii) People have different wants (Assumption 3).

(iv) Hence, the more decision-makers, the more inconsistent wants and the more inconsistent (conflicting) decisions (Implication).

(v) A decision is a kind of conflict-resolution (*Ex def.*).

(vi) Hence, the more contradictory decisions, the more unresolved conflicts and the fewer actual decisions are being made (Implication).

(vii) Hence, the fewer the decision-makers, the more actual decisions will be made.

Sample Theorem

The more decision-makers in a political system, the more decisions will be made.

Proof

(i) A decision is the abandonment of one or more alternatives (*Ex def.*).

(ii) Thus, the more available alternatives, the more potential decisions (Implication).

(iii) People have different wants (Assumption 3).

(iv) Hence, the more people making decisions, the more available alternatives (Implication).

(v) Hence, the more decision-makers, the more decisions.

Sample Theorem

The fewer decision-makers in a political system, the fewer decisions made.

Proof

(i) The more people belonging to a political system, the more available alternatives (wants) (Assumption 3).

(ii) People differ in their wants (Assumption 3).

(iii) Hence, the fewer decision-makers, the fewer the wants that tend to be employed in decision-making (Implication).

(iv) Hence, the fewer the alternatives, the fewer the decisions that will be made.

Sample Theorem

The more decision-makers in a political system, the fewer decisions will be made.

Proof

(i) There is a limited amount of energy in the political system (Assumption 8).

(ii) The more decision-makers, the more alternatives (wants) (Implication).

(iii) A decision is the abandonment of alternatives (*Ex def.*).

(iv) Each decision costs something in energy (Assumption 8).

(v) Hence (from Step i), the average amount of energy left per decision is less with each decision made.

(vi) Yet, an average quantity of energy is necessary for the making of each decision (Assumption 8).

(vii) And thus, if less energy is available per average decision, fewer decisions will be made.

(viii) Therefore, more decision-makers will produce fewer decisions.

Problems

1. Using the discussion of political decision in the text, in which it is pointed out that lack of knowledge about what people want may affect a politician's decisions, what might be the social consequences if a politician learned about the results of an actual poll presented below?

RESPONSE OF URBAN WORKING-CLASS SAMPLE

Statement	Percentage Who Agree
"Politics and government are getting so complicated that the average person can't really understand what's really going on."	73%
"The way people vote is the main thing that decides how things are run in this country."	74%

2. A political scientist (Professor Warner Schilling of Columbia University) has pointed out that President Truman, by ordering the Atomic Energy Commission and the military to go ahead and experiment with a hydrogen bomb in 1949 and 1950, avoided making a decision. That is, President Truman avoided saying, "No, we are not going to make an H-bomb, and that's that," by saying, "Let's see if our scientists can do it, and *then* (if they can) we'll decide whether we want to produce the bombs." Had President Truman made a decision as that term is used in this book? Why or why not?

3. Kaplan's Law declares: "A child with a hammer always finds something to pound." How does this principle apply to the behavior of politicians, office-holders, bureaucrats, dissidents, and the average citizen?

Suggested Readings

David Braybrooke, *Three Tests for Democracy* (1968).
Robert A. Dahl and Charles E. Lindblom, *Politics, Economics, and Welfare* (1953).
C. J. Friedrich (ed.), "Rational Decision," *Nomos* 7: Rational Decision (1964).
Arnold Heidenkeimer, *Political Corruption* (1970).
Irving L. Janis, "Decisional Conflicts: A Theoretical Analysis," *Journal of Conflict Resolution* 3 (1959).
Charles E. Lindblom and David Braybrooke, *A Strategy of Decision* (1963).
Warner R. Schilling, "The H-Bomb Decision: How to Decide without Actually Choosing," *Political Science Quarterly,* Vol. 76, p. 37, (March, 1961).
Herbert Simon, *Administrative Behavior* (1947).
Judith Sklar, "Decision Theories," *Nomos* 7: Rational Decision (1964).
Richard C. Snyder, H. Bruck, and B. Sapin, *Foreign Policy Decision-Making* (1962).
D. A. Strickland, *Scientists in Politics* (1968).

CHAPTER 4

Conflict

One way to begin the study of conflict is to understand that without conflict there is no politics. If everybody suddenly decided to quit fighting and always cooperate, the political scientists would be put out of business. Only historians would then be hired in order to study past conflict.

A CONFLICT is what happens when two things which cannot be had at the same time are wanted at the same time. This is different from an *illusion,* where something is wanted which cannot be had at all. It is not too different from *indecision,* where a person is unable to decide *which* thing he wants. In a conflict, the emphasis is more on the fact that he wants *both* things and is pained by the fact that they do not fit together.

A conflict exists in an individual human being when, for example, a person wants to get up in the morning but *also* wants to get more sleep. Conflicts exist in human groups and organizations when some people in a group cannot compromise with other people in the group. For instance, if some people in a club want to go on a picnic to the ocean and others want to go camping in the mountains, there is a conflict within the group. When Romeo and Tybalt fought their duel, it was a conflict because each wanted to survive *and* to kill the other.

Some conflicts result in *violence;* but not all violence stems from human conflicts. In ancient times, people used to explain natural violence (e.g., storms and earthquakes) by saying that it was caused by the gods or by conflicts among the gods. In the *Iliad,* one reads about "Zeus the Thunderer" and "Poseidon the Earthshaker." In that story, the gods also dabble in the military conflict between the Greeks and Trojans, just as Jehovah took the side of the Hebrew children by sending awful plagues against Pharaoh (*Exodus* 5:11).

Violence means the bodily harming of human beings. This is so shocking and repulsive to most people—the *very idea* is so upsetting—that man needs elaborate justifications and diversions to deaden his thoughts and memories of violence. Though government is often defined as the people who have a "monopoly on violence" in a society, it is remarkable that most of the language of politics is about the *prospects* or *probabilities* of violence: one sees, therefore, many vague references to aggressions, threats, preemptions, provocations, ultimatums, aggravations, and the like. In other words, most of what is heard about politics is tainted with violence without quite *being* violence. In this respect, politics is no different from war movies and Westerns—dozens of people getting killed or wounded each night on the TV, quite realistically—and politics serves the same (melodramatic) purpose.

War is the most violent kind of political conflict. It *is* a *political* conflict because by threatening war, or by starting a war, one country is trying to get another to do what the latter was not willing to do without being forced. The violence and bloodshed and destruction of war show how badly some people can want things that other people do not want and will not do. Of course, there are people who *want* conflict because they enjoy fighting, find it exciting, or are mad about something else. Mercenaries, who are not notorious for their avoidance of conflict, were an important force in the wars of Biafra and the Congo. Likewise, there were foreign troops and "volunteers" in the Indo-China war who may have found the experience exhilarating.

Most political conflict, however, is not so violent. Most of it follows rules (even war follows rules sometimes), and it is possible to tell pretty much what a political system will be like from day to day. (People get bored so easily that they like to pretend that they cannot tell what the political system will be like. Thus, when they have nothing else to do, some people engage in alarming activities—threats, accusations, denunciations, fabulous promises and prophesies, and so on—in order to make the political system look more interesting and less predictable.)

There are, of course, political conflicts that result from so-called "structural" inconsistencies, such as division of profits among various occupational groupings, overlapping ambitions of ethnic or religious groups, and competition between certain lifestyles (class conflict). There are, to be sure, conflicts that stem from personal envy and rivalry, or from family feuds and long-standing regional chauvinism. And there are in any population vague resentments and discontents that are expressed through defiance of laws, police, and bureaucratic regulation. An interesting theoretical question is which of these conflicts can or should be brought under control, and which are "basic" to the human situation and therefore intractable.

Some of the rules that control conflict in the political system are found in writings, like constitutions, laws, judicial decisions, and the regulations of agencies. Other rules are taught by word of mouth to newcomers and may be different in different parts of the country, in different parts of the political system, or among different groups and classes of people.

It is *very important* to realize that there are many different sets of rules and that people often disagree about which rules apply to which situations. It is not unknown for people who are losing in a conflict to complain that the ones who are winning are breaking the rules. There are people who believe that *their* rules for political behavior are God's rules. It is not surprising that people who always lose under the present rules would want to change the rules regarding conflict, or that those who always win would see such changes as bad and would see any refusal to follow the rules as bad.

People who want to keep the rules of political conflict unchanged are called *conservatives*. People who want to change a few of the rules are usually called *liberals*. People who want to change a lot of rules, or some of the more important rules, are called *revolutionaries*. People who would like to do away with all rules are called *anarchists*. Conservatives and liberals view each other as bad; they view revolutionaries as very bad; revolutionaries view them as very bad; they all consider anarchists to be pretty bad, especially if there are very many of them; and so on.

People who are not too excited and angry about their own rules can often avoid conflicts by asking: "What is it that we want to get done with these rules?" It may be that both sides in the conflict want to get the same thing done and that the thing over which they accidentially ended up in conflict was the *rules!* Needless to say, in most political conflicts, people are fully aware that they want different things and that there will have to be a loser. Two people may want to be President in a political system that does not provide for more than one President at a time. Or some people may want radio, television, and all government publications to be only in French, while other people in the same country want them to be only in English.

PEACE results when conflict is forgotten or given up. There are people who claim that human beings will never be able to give up conflict. If this is true, it is still possible that people might be able to give up some kinds of conflicts (e.g., wars) in exchange for others (e.g., boxing matches or bullfights). If people are really incapable of avoiding the more spectacular and destructive kinds of conflicts, obviously there is never going to be peace in the international political system.

In some ways, conflict is much more exciting than peace. People who have, for this reason, made conflict into a habit will not want to give it up; they will think that a person who wants them to "give up" something is trying to start *another* conflict. They will then start a fight over this or some other issue; and that will prove, to them, that peace is impossible. It will also prove to everybody that peace cannot exist for the time being.

When two or more people exchange promises, they are making a CONTRACT. Usually each party is promising to give up something in exchange for something given up by the other party. Contracts are obviously examples of *cooperation* and, as such, have a special and limited place in political analysis.

Cooperation in its simple forms—as, for example, between lovers, business partners, or co-authors—has nothing at all to do with politics. Cooperation (in particular, contract) is mentioned here because it may provide either (1) an *occasion* for conflict or (2) a *technique* for improving one's chances of winning.

(1) Since there is no promise that cannot be broken, you can always start a fight by breaking your promise or by claiming the other guy broke (or plans to break) his promise. You can also start a fight when some *other people* are cooperating with one another, on the grounds that they are doing so to get ahead of you.

(2) Likewise, you *might* in fact be cooperating in order to improve your chances of winning some conflict or other. Menelaus and Agamemnon got a lot of other Greeks to join them in their attempt to bring Helen home from Troy. The Crusades featured a good deal of cooperation, too. In modern times, there are such alliances as the Warsaw Pact or the North Atlantic Treaty Organization. There have *even* been cases where cooperation was used as a *deception* so that someone else would *think* that a peaceable contract was being made. Thus, the poor Trojans believed that the Greeks were making a peace offering when they gave them the famous gift-horse. Faking is an important part of modern political practice; and even in democratic countries it makes up more than half of the political behavior.

People have always longed for a world in which cooperation and freedom of contract would replace conflict. It is interesting that not only the great religions but also the humanists, communists, and anarchists want this. But as long as contracts continue to cause, as well as to heal, conflicts, political analysis will have to deal with the subject. (Political analysis can be buried, as a dead science, just as soon as the cheering stops, the fighting is given up, the corpses are removed, and the grievances forgotten.)

Conflict occurs in different social forums, which is to say that the elements of conflict can vary. Two people may want to be president of a college fraternity. Members will decide the issue using certain "rules of thumb": they will ask themselves which candidate is the most glamorous, who has assumed the greatest responsibility in the past, who has done whom the most favors? Here there is a conflict over individuals or *personalities.* Such conflicts, while important to the people involved, do not usually capture the headlines, and for a very good reason. This is true because it is conflict involving whole social *categories* (e.g., castes, classes, regions, elites, masses, religions, races, occupations), as well as individuals, which engages most public attention. Furthermore, such conflicts are often over important policies, such as which people are going to rule, who is going to obey, to whom will people look up, and on whom will people look down. Of course, the conflict may or may not be expressed in such terms (see Chapter 6), but actually that's what it's all about.

The kind of *agents* (see Chapter 7) that people have will indicate a great deal about how conflict is expressed and, especially, about how obvious it is. In political systems where everybody is watched closely by the authorities who have most of the power, conflict is usually hushed up. Newspapers are not allowed to print stories about policy disagreements, although sometimes they will be allowed to dispute how *efficiently* the bureaucrats are carrying out the elite's policy. (By allowing disagreements over means, but not over ends, the people get a chance to drain off their aggressions and to think that they live in a tolerant political system.)

The authorities, then, can quiet down *open conflict,* but they cannot always get rid of hidden or *closed conflict.* Indicators of closed conflict are things like cabals, conspiracies, spies, secret police, "overseas" patriots who propagandize against the regime from a safe distance, crime, suicides, or subtle non-political digs made against the regime by writers, composers, or movie producers. However, because everything in a political system affects everything else, hidden conflict can be very important. In fact, just when conflict seems to have disappeared, it will often break out into the open.

Open conflict would include conflicts that are well-known and openly discussed like wars and elections. Elections are wars which are fought with "ballots rather than bullets." They do not break out into violence in stable political systems because the conflict is within the accepted rules of the game; wars are about the rules themselves. When one leaves out things like wars, open conflict is the kind of conflict found in democracies (even though there may be conspiracies in democracies, the system itself is not a conspiracy). In fact, there could not be a democracy if people could not bring their discontent and demands out into the open. Even so, there are always some demands that you cannot make, even in a democracy; you can try to do so, but you run the risk of getting told to shut-up in no uncertain terms.

Violence, money, time, skill, associations, propaganda, votes, and reputations are all weapons that are used in politics to get what people want. They are political resources.

Political resources are those means by which an individual is able to gain access to and influence decisions in favor of his wants. In our society most, if not all, resources are viewed as scarce. In other words, the more of one resource an individual has (e.g., money), the less of the same resource the next individual will have. All of these resources are unevenly distributed among the population. An *uneven distribution* means that some members have more than others.

Distribution is cumulative when to gain in one resource means at the same time to gain in other resources. Distribution is non-cumulative when a gain in one resource does not mean a gain in any other resource.

It is often found that the distribution of resources is both uneven and non-cumulative. That is, a man with a lot of *money* will not necessarily possess a high degree of *political knowledge;* nor will a man with a lot of money and political knowledge necessarily have enough of the resource of *time* to be politically effective in a conflict situation. He may spend a large amount of his time investing his money and very few such hours in obtaining political outcomes. In fact, such a man may not perceive the relationship between making money and the political processes.

We have just mentioned one of the most valuable resources in politics—time. Time is a valuable resource in two major respects: (1) the amount of time an individual can spend influencing the political system, and (2) the amount of time the leaders (agents) can spend allocating values. Most men can only think and talk about one problem at a time. Influence often takes a lot of talk or persuasion—thus time is of vital importance to the individual who wants to get his political demands heard by the effective leaders (agents).

Time is important to the leader who has to process the demands. Since he can only attend to one of them at a time, it is quite easy to overload him. Thus, one can say that the more time leaders have, the more demands they can process and the more solutions (alternatives) they can propose. Also, the more time the agents have, and the fewer problems they encounter, the more possible solutions they can figure out. Still further, the more leaders a system has, the more time it has, since leaders can specialize in specific areas. However, the more leaders there are, the greater the chance of misunderstanding, and the greater the chance of misunderstanding, the more likely conflict is to occur.

Money—economic wealth—serves both as a political and economic, as well as a social and cultural, resource in most societies of the world. Wealth commands all other resources.

Money spent on political ends has a different value for different people. This individual value is *utility*. The utility of a dollar spent on politics for the Negro poor is probably greatly different than the utility of a dollar spent on politics by an Astor or a Rockefeller. Thus, the utility of different values is unevenly distributed among people.

Time has this same property. Some men may place a higher utility on time spent playing golf than other men do. Thus, an individual with a lot of time on his hands may decide to utilize that time in apolitical pursuits and be ineffective politically, despite the fact that he has a great deal of money to spend on greens fees. (However, it must be pointed out that the man who spends his time and money on golf may be allocating political values in terms of defining the situation where golf courses will be maintained instead of houses for the poor.) Thus, the rich man, because of his utility rankings, may be politically ineffective. Another man, with a lot of time but few dollars, may use his time by attending city council meetings rather than playing golf.

He in turn may be much more effective than the man with a lot of money. Thus, one can say: the more time a man has, despite his income, the more effective he *may* be in obtaining desired political alternatives.

Another resource, *skill,* comes from apprenticeship, the understanding of how the world really works, and practice. Skill is harder to get than other resources because (1) it takes a lot of effort, practice, and patience over long periods of time before it produces anything and (2) it requires that a person give up all his wishful thinking, admit his ignorance, and pay attention only to the details of reality. Obviously people who are already nervous about their pride are able neither to become humble, to give up their dreams of glory, nor to relax long enough to learn difficult skills. Nonetheless, the development of skills is the only way the political system can become more effective in satisfying wants.

Probably most people would like to engage in politics without violence. To get this, they usually prefer that somebody (the regime) possess a monopoly of violence in the community. (Some few people, who do not really count in politics as we know it, think that no one, ever, should have any control over the means of violence. They would even disarm the government.) When one has located the group that has the greatest capacity for violence (e.g., controls the most guns, warships, and the like), he has located the "government" or the "state." Governments do not have to be set up in fancy buildings, and governmental leaders do not have to be called president, king, tsar, senator, or what have you. If a gang of bandits controls a given area and a given number of people, then it is the government. When no one controls the preponderance of force, as in the international system, then war is more likely to occur (as long as people think as they do today), simply because many people with different wants have some say over the use of force.

Since the government has most of the available force, it normally does not have to use force against a direct threat. Of course, it will use force very often against others who break the rules of the game, like hoodlums, dope addicts, and others. The government especially will not have to use force if (1) most of the people like the government, (2) think it *should* have most of the force available, and (3) if the government satisfies some of the needs of the people.

People can be hurt or wounded in many ways and not only by being hurt physically. To be attacked in a speech or classroom, to have one's ideas dismissed as "silly," and so forth, can hurt people inside and affect their self-esteem. *Identification* also involves possible wounds. Some college professors do not like it when somebody attacks "the intellectuals," even though nobody has ever accused *them* of being intellectuals. Republicans do not always like it when a Republican President is attacked by the Democrats, and vice versa. Thus, when something or somebody a person likes is attacked, he sometimes acts as if *he* had been attacked. These wounds amount to "psychological violence," or the intimidation, mortification, and disorganization of people's self-conceptions. Since the ability of people to pursue their interests and protect themselves is dependent on a healthy self-conception, psychological violence often results in physical and economic losses as well.

The larger, more stable, and more complex a political system is, the less important personalities (single individuals) are and the more important associations (many individuals) are as political resources (see Chapter 8). Political associations are like political armies; even though they may not use guns to get what they want, they do use other weapons. Political parties and interest groups are the typical political associations of our times, and their number often determines the kind of conflict that results. In two-party parliamentary systems, for example, some conflict has been resolved even before the representatives meet (such as which party will elect the prime minister); in multi-party systems, coalition governments are often elected after the representatives meet to make trades and deals of all sorts. Thus, conflict may be more open in multi-party systems. One-party systems tend to reduce open conflict even more.

As one thinks about all these types and sizes of conflict, it is desirable to keep in mind that conflict is part of a somewhat more general human experience—*trouble.* One kind of trouble results when things erupt which no one especially *wants,* things which show that something is wrong though no one knows how to prevent or cure it. A second kind is trouble sought intentionally for such motives as gain, excitement, enhancement of self-esteem, and so on. A third kind of trouble is that which comes as a *surprise* to the rulers, when, for instance, new demands and conflicts appear in the political system and the leaders must try to adapt their old rules to a situation the likes of which never arose before in that system. If some of the people in the political system view the trouble as 'fate' or 'nature,' and others view it as the result of somebody's intention or fault, then new conflicts will arise: one group will talk about putting an end to the trouble by winning, losing, trying harder, getting mobilized, and the like; and the others will talk about averting the trouble, accepting it, making it a way of life, and so on. One can readily see what these two, very different views of trouble have to do with the chances of agreeing on various ways of resolving conflicts.

Sample Theorem

The more conflict within a group, the greater the decision latitude of the leadership.

Proof

(i) People have different wants (Assumption 3).

(ii) Decision is the abandoning of some alternatives (*Ex def.*).

(iii) Conflict exists when there are incompatible wants (*Ex def.*, Ch. 3).

(iv) Therefore, the more conflict there is in a group, the more incompatible wants there must necessarily be (Implication).

(v) The more incompatible wants present, the more decisions can be made (Implication).

(vi) In any group the leadership is that part of the membership that usually makes decisions (*Ex def.*).

(vii) And hence, the more conflict within a group, the more decisions the leaders will be able to make, and, thus, the more decision latitude they will have.

Sample Theorem

In a political system where each individual wants several different things, and different individuals want different things, there can be no political agreement and there will be conflict (Arrow's paradox, modified and extended).

Proof

(i) If there were "perfect agreement" between individual 1 and individual 2, they would want the same thing(s) and would *not* want (i.e., reject) the same thing(s) (*Ex def.*).

(ii) If individual 1 wants A most, B next, and C least and if individual 2 wants C most, A next, and B least, then there is no agreement. (*Both* 1 *and* 2 do not want A most, or C most, or C least, or B least, or B or A next most; nor do they both want any combination of AB, CA, etc.)

(iii) Thus, if most individuals in the political system want more than two different things, in different orders of preference, there can be no agreement.

(iv) If the wants are truly different, they will be non-consistent.

(v) And, where people want different, non-consistent things, there is conflict (*Ex def.*).

Sample Theorem

Even where people have the same wants, but differ in the *amounts* they want, there may be conflict.

Proof

(i) Wants are limited and can be satisfied only in a limited number of ways (Assumptions 3 and 8).

(ii) If one person wants more than half of something and a second person also wants more than half of that thing, there can be no agreement without one or both of them taking a loss (Implication).

(iii) In such a case, a conflict exists (*ex. def.*) because two things (more than half of the same thing × 2) are wanted which cannot be had, or because each person himself wants two things (to win and to compromise) which cannot be had at the same time.

Problems

1. There are many kinds of political conflicts. You may have noticed that when the conflict over who was going to be mayor in your city was concluded, things went on pretty much as before so far as most people were concerned, especially if there were no serious issues involved in the campaign. This would be an example of conflict over *personalities*. Some political conflict, however, occurs over *issues* which affect many more people than just the politicians who win or lose public office. Thus, medicare, urban renewal, and civil rights conflicts can affect millions of people. But if such issues are handled in traditional ways (i.e., if they are settled the way people have come to expect them to be settled), then the *norms* of the society have not been violated and people can usually accept the outcome of the conflict. Sometimes, however, people disagree completely about politics: about personalities, about issues, about norms, and more importantly, about *values*. For example, you may want democracy, or the right to vote for competing politicians at regular intervals; someone else may want fascism, or rule by some "natural" elite; someone else may want communism, or the dictatorship of the proletariat, at least in the short run. This would be a very serious conflict indeed since it is a disagreement over values. In Figure 3, the "conflict line" can be manipulated to show the levels of conflict that may exist in society. What would be the likely consequence of the level of conflict indicated for Society One? What would be likely to happen in Society Two, given its "conflict line?"

2. In October, 1962, country A discovered through espionage that country B was locating missile-launching equipment and missiles in country C. Country C was close enough to country A that missiles of this kind could easily and accurately

FIGURE 3. LEVELS OF CONFLICT

Society One		
Values		
Norms		
Issues		
Personalities		← Conflict Line
Consensus		Conflict

Society Two		
Conflict Line →	Values	
	Norms	
	Issues	
	Personalities	
Consensus		Conflict

reach several major cities in country A, including the capital city. The leader of country A became very alarmed, demanded that country B take its missiles home, and sent out warships which, he said, would stop B's ships from bringing any more missiles to C. (a) Describe what had happened in the language of this chapter. (b) Forgetting that you know how this crisis came out, list all the ways it might *possibly* have come out.

3. Presidents in America have often had campaign slogans ("A chicken in every pot," "He kept us out of war," and so on) and lately have had names for their Administrations ("the New Deal," "the Fair Deal," "the New Frontier," "the Great Society"). They have also had special names for special programs. Some names, such as "the Marshall Plan," come from the person who thought up or publicized the idea; some, like "the War on Poverty," are supposed to describe the purpose of the program; but the names are always intended to sound attractive and appealing.

One President came up with a program that he called "Atoms for Peace." It was supposed to make atomic energy available to other countries in order to show that the U.S. believes in peace and to get the Soviet Union to cooperate in setting up an international atomic energy agency. Some of the people working for this President were alarmed because they thought that giving atomic materials to more and more countries would make it more likely (since the same materials could be used to make bombs) that an atomic war could get started. These people probably would have called the program "Atoms against Peace," which *would not* have been an appealing title. (a) What might happen to these people, within the President's own administration, if they made loud, public criticisms of the "Atoms for Peace" program? (b) What if the President had gotten so excited about the idea that he announced it without consulting any of the experts, who later persuaded him it was a very dangerous idea. How might he change his opinion and get out of the proposal? (c) What if the allies of the U.S. heard that the Administration was split on "Atoms for Peace" and that one group wanted to give atomic materials to all other countries and another group was working to defeat or reverse this policy? How would that affect the allies' trust in U.S. promises to protect them with atomic weapons and in the U.S. advice that they would not need to make atomic bombs themselves?

Suggested Readings

Raymond Aron, *On War* (1959).
Kenneth Boulding. *Conflict and Defense* (1962).
A. H. Buss, *The Psychology of Aggression* (1961).
Sigmund Freud, *Civilization and Its Discontents* (1929).
Mahatma K. Gandhi, *Satyagraha: Non-Violent Resistance* (1961).
Thomas Hobbes, *Leviathan* (1651).
Gabriel Kolko, *The Politics of War* (1968).
Harold D. Lasswell, *Politics: Who Gets What, When, How* (1958).
B. H. Liddell-Hart, *Strategy* (1954).
Konrad Lorenz, *On Aggression* (1966).
Niccolo Machiavelli, *The Prince* (1513).
Karl Marx, *The Civil War in France* (1871).
Anatol Rapoport, *Fights, Games, and Debates* (1960).
L. Richardson, *Statistics of Deadly Quarrels* (1960).
E. E. Schattschneider, *The Semi-Sovereign People* (1960).
Thomas Schelling, *The Strategy of Conflict* (1960).
W. Shakespeare, *Romeo and Juliet,* Act III, Scene 1 (1597).
Georg Simmel, *Conflict* (1955).
Georges Sorel, *Reflections on Violence* (1925).
J. D. Williams, *The Compleat Strategyst* (1954).
Quincy Wright, *A Study of War* (1965).

CHAPTER 5

Conflict-Resolution

Anything that puts an end to a conflict or makes it into a smaller conflict is a CONFLICT-RESOLUTION.

A common type of conflict-resolution is to walk away from the conflict. Anything that separates a person from the trouble is an act of CONFLICT-AVOIDANCE. Conflict-avoidance is a kind of conflict-resolution, since it puts the conflict out of the picture. This can be done by walking away from the conflict, by postponing it, by refusing to think about it, and so on. If country A refuses to enter a war on the side of country B, its ally, then country A is practicing conflict-avoidance.

In politics, as in other activities, it may be that conflict-avoidance only *temporarily* resolves the conflict. For instance, country A might discover that a world war got started because it refused to come to the assistance of its ally B; or country A might discover that during the time its leaders refused to think about its own racial conflicts, they had become so serious that it *could not* avoid them later.

Another common variety of conflict-resolution is compromise. COMPROMISE happens when the people who want x and the people who want y agree to accept z instead. The solution, z, may be somewhere in between x and y $\left(\text{e.g., } z = \dfrac{x + y}{2} \right)$, or it may be something separate (e.g., where the people who want everybody in the country to speak French and the people who want everybody to speak German agree, instead, that everybody should speak Latin). Political compromises are easier to arrange where there are few people living in the disputed area, as in Greenland or Antarctica.

Some compromises are decisions to postpone a decision. People may feel that at a future time their opponent will be weaker. They may feel that a fight at this time is too risky for themselves or the political system. Sometimes people already have in mind a compromise when they enter into a conflict; that is, they hope that some alternative reward will turn up and provide the opportunity for compromise and the pleasure of "making-up."

A third kind of conflict-resolution is capitulation. CAPITULATION is the result when the people who want x and the people who want y agree to accept y. For example, in war one country may surrender to another; in local politics the people who want better public parks may agree to live peaceably with the majority of the community even though the majority do not want better public parks. Capitulation is a risky kind of conflict-resolution because there is always the possibility that the people who lose out will want to "get even" somehow. In politics, much energy is expended so that capitulations will look more like compromises or so that the losers will not appear to be too weak and will not feel looked down upon. This can be done (1) if the losers pretend that they really wanted to lose all along, (2) if the losers escape after losing and go somewhere else to live, (3) if the winners confer some honors or benefits on the losers, (4) if the winners claim that they just barely won, or (5) if the losers join the winners and believe that *they too are the winners!*

Fate-control is another kind of conflict-resolution. FATE-CONTROL exists when part or all of the conflict is changed so that the people involved can no longer help themselves—since they can no longer help themselves, they cannot be expected to compromise or capitulate. The following are examples. (a) Country A might be able to make a machine (the so-called "doomsday machine") which would automatically make the whole world blow up if country B attacked country A. (b) A political leader might have such a bad temper that whenever people did what he did not want, he would lose control of himself and wouldn't be able to continue the conflict according to the usual rules. (c) When two women both claimed that a certain child belonged to them, King Solomon threatened to cut the child in half; if he had done so, he would have resolved the conflict by making it impossible for *either* to get what she wanted.

The scope and quality of a conflict can be altered by mystification. MYSTIFICATION is anything that will keep secret a person's actual behavior or intentions. The easiest method is to "keep your mouth shut." If, however, the truth slips out, it can be buried again by denying it, saying several other things rapidly, changing the subject, or attacking someone else on moral grounds. The political uses of mystification are quite familiar: it keeps military secrets out of the hands of enemies; it gives the leaders time to consider issues about which they have not yet made up their minds; it prevents the followers from getting the information they need to criticize the leaders or to get an effective opposition movement going; it permits the leaders to wait and see how things turn out (then interpret their vague statements after the fact); and it impresses some of the followers because they think the silence or the fancy phrases of the leaders are signs of "dignity" (see *credenda* and *miranda,* p. 66). In the United States during the year before a Presidential election, one will hear people who want to be President saying that they do not want to be President or saying puzzling, vague, meaningless things. This is usually not because they cannot think straight or are struggling with new and profound thoughts; it is because they want to see what kind of support they are going to get before publicly announcing their intentions. So, when asked to say something, they just utter some words. This sort of behavior is not limited to politicians by any means; but they are, as a rule, rather good at it.

Clarity is avoided in politics because it reduces the number of *apparent* choices. Facing the facts is avoided because it means discovering that there are fewer *actual* choices than we dream there are. People prefer dreaming their fuzzy old pipe-dreams instead of getting definite and doing something about the world. Hence, they rather like the politician who will warm up the fuzzy old pipe-dreams for them.

Over the centuries, there have been people who have tried to get what they wanted in ways that were not normally accepted in their political system. Some have used or threatened to use violent means (REVOLUTION). Some have refused to have anything to do with the political system or as little to do with it as they could (NON-PARTICIPATION). Some have gotten in the way of the decision-makers so that it would become more difficult or expensive to carry out decisions (CIVIL DISOBEDIENCE). Non-participation and civil disobedience are used by people who assume that it will make the decision-makers feel bad to use force, or that the decision-makers would rather give in than pay the costs of using force, or both. People also use non-participation and civil disobedience to call attention to their wants, knowing that the authorities have to pay a lot of attention to anyone they *make* participate in a political system or *make* get out of the way.

Some degree of non-participation is practiced by everyone, no matter who he is or in what society he lives. Sleep is the clearest example of non-participation practiced by all human beings. People who suffer nervous breakdowns and remain mentally ill over long periods of time are also often non-participants in the political system. When a person places a high value on non-participation (e.g., being left alone to pursue a hobby or to go on a picnic with his sweetheart), he is apt to praise it as *privacy;* when he places a low value on it, he is apt to condemn it as *irresponsibility,* shirking, frivolity, or laziness. Political systems—and social systems in all respects—are quite different from one another when it comes to letting individuals alone. Behavior that in one society is regarded as "minding your own business" is regarded in another society as the worst sort of grumpiness, loneliness, or even psychosis. Hence, people who in the U.S. system feel that they are being denied their civil liberties and persecuted by the authorities might be regarded in other systems as being either too timid about insisting on their right of privacy against the government or as inventing excuses for not cooperating like everybody else.

When people in a conflict agree to follow somebody else's solution for ending the conflict, the procedure is called ARBITRATION. Arbitration is different from MEDIATION, which is the process whereby the conflicting people agree to let somebody else *suggest* solutions to the conflict. Mediation and arbitration are interesting examples of how conflicts can be changed—and sometimes resolved—by changing the number of people involved. No doubt, it is also possible to get into new conflicts and to make the original conflict worse by adding more participants. In a political system where judges end up sending murderers to jail, for example, arbitration probably reduces the amount of conflict. But in political systems where the murderers can escape from jail and commit more crimes (perhaps injuring the judge to get even with him), arbitration does not reduce the number of conflicts.

Although it may not look like any sort of a *solution* to a conflict, a stalemate *can* turn out to be a conflict-resolution. A STALEMATE occurs when none of the people in a conflict is able or willing to do anything to bring it to an end. If country A and country B both want Sinai to be part of *their* country, and neither will back down, but neither will attack the other, it could go on for years that way. The longer it goes on that way and does not get any worse, the more likely it is that people will get used to it and accept *it* as a solution.

The reason there are not any conflict-resolutions that will solve all conflicts and prevent any more from arising is that people change their wants, want things that other people also want, and want things that cannot be had.

Sample Theorem

In a conflict, the person who can control the choice of authorities or who can control the definition of the conflict, controls its outcome (Schattschneider's law).

Proof

(i) Only a limited number of conflict-resolving mechanisms can be employed in any political system (Assumption 8).

(ii) These mechanisms involve or depend on the authorities (*Ex def.* Political System).

(iii) All of these mechanisms, or sets thereof, provide different and sometimes inconsistent outcomes (Inspection of Chapter on Conflict-Resolution).

(iv) In any political system, people have definite ideas as to which authorities and which conflict-resolutions are *acceptable* for different types of conflicts (Assumptions 3, 4, and 6).

(v) Since there is a limited number of acceptable resolutions (Step iv) and since different resolutions produce different outcomes (Step iii), whatever determines the form of conflict-resolution determines the outcome of the conflict.

(vi) Therefore, if a person can determine the *manner* in which a conflict will be processed, he can determine its outcome.

Sample Theorem

If the parties to a political conflict try to resolve it, each using a different method, the status quo will be the solution.

Proof

(i) The *methods* of conflict-resolution are discrete and non-consistent (*Ex def.* and previous Theorem).

(ii) The parties to a political conflict are seeking different outcomes (i.e., want different, non-consistent things) (*Ex def.*).

(iii) A party to a conflict would not knowlingly choose a method that would produce an outcome he did not want (Assumption 1).

(iv) Hence, the difference in methods of conflict-resolution excludes an agreement on outcome (Schattschneider's law, above).

(v) Since, in the absence of an agreed-upon resolution of the conflict, things remain as they were, the outcome is the status quo. (Paradox: To fail is to choose the status quo. The status quo *is* a disagreement and one which gave rise to a conflict. Thus, to fail to agree is to choose to disagree. Thus, not to agree *is* to agree.)

Problems

1. Suppose you knew three people who were very sure of their beliefs. Suppose that one person was a businessman who refused to read good books about economics, another person was a Communist who studied only Marxist social science, and the last person was a member of a religious organization and refused to read any books that had not been "approved" by his church's newspaper. Using the above analysis of conflict-resolution, what might account for the behavior of these people?

2. Some social scientists talk about the "strain toward agreement" and the "separation anxiety" that exists among many people. What they are saying is that some people, for different reasons, do not like conflict. Thus, some people prefer to stop rather than to continue fighting among each other. Suppose that two individuals who disagree about some issue fear even more strongly that they may not reach agreement concerning the issue. Suppose, also, that no one else wants to get involved (they do not like conflict either!). What will be the likely outcome of the conflict if both parties to the conflict suffer from a "separation anxiety?" What will be the outcome if only one of the parties suffers from such anxiety?

3. Conflict that exists between, say, two countries is really conflict between the politicians of two countries; each nation's politicians want the other nation's politicians to do something that the latter does not want to do. In an effort to change the minds of the other countries' politicians, each side may increase its "power" by building more nuclear weapons, stationing more soldiers on the borders of the other country, and so forth. If the conflict is between two very powerful countries, the chances of arbitration and/or mediation are small. This is so because both such means of conflict-resolution depend upon power equal to

or greater than the power of those involved in the conflict. (a) Assuming that the "power" of each nation in a conflict situation is roughly equal and that their differences are not major (i.e., neither side wants the other side to change a great deal), how will the conflict be resolved? (b) Now suppose everything is the same except that each side wants the other side to change very much. (c) Assuming that both sides want to avoid war, how will the conflict be resolved?

4. During the 1890s in the United States, many poor white farmers in the Midwest joined with poor white and Negro farmers in the South and demanded that the government "do something" about their economic conditions. Certain politicians who represented the more well-to-do groups began to "wave the bloody shirt," that is, began to convince the poor white farmers that they should not join with Negroes in a political movement but should, rather, work with the well-to-do whites. Thus, conflict between wealthy and poor whites was resolved. Which of the conflict-resolution processes discussed in the text worked in this case?

5. Suggest what possible outcomes might occur in the following situation:

A group of businessmen in a small community owns two pieces of land which would be most profitable if they could be sold to government agencies as sites for new buildings. These businessmen also want to build better schools and make the school system attractive to outside industries. A group of mothers in the community wants a new school. The mothers intensely feel that the school should be located at least a mile away from the land owned by the above-mentioned businessmen. The businessmen feel that the school is more important than selling their land; but they would like to have both things. The mothers feel that having the school built in their part of town is more important than any other decision to improve the educational system. The businessmen know that if they get a school built, no matter where, they will get the contracts to build it and to supply the new building.

In describing the outcomes, comment on (a) which side won or lost and (b) what it was they won or lost.

6. In 1798 the Federalist Party controlled the central government and passed the Alien and Sedition Acts which prohibited, among other things, any person from writing or publishing "any false, scandalous and malicious writings against the government of the United States. . . ." Seven years earlier, the First Amendment had been adopted; it states that "Congress shall make no laws . . . abridging the freedom of speech, or of the press. . . ." Now, if you had to prove that the Alien and Sedition Acts were consistent with the First Amendment (that is, that they were not unconstitutional and that it *does* make sense to talk about sedition in a country that guarantees the freedom of speech and the press), what arguements would you offer?

7. The United States refused for over 20 years to recognize the Communist regime that governed China since 1949. What factor(s) in this chapter is (are) relevant to that fact?

8. In political negotiations and bargaining, it is often difficult to get the parties to say what positions they took earlier in the negotiation. (The reason is that they want to emphasize what they now agree on, or their present claims, without unnecessary wrangling or appearance of hypocrisy.) What if you knew, however, that A, which had at first said it would never permit its bases in Antartica to be inspected by B, now says that it has finally persuaded B to permit mutual inspection of Antartic bases. What would A's maneuver be called?

9. Boulding's Law (deriving from Lewis Carroll) states, "The more for you, the less for me." This is not (as everyone knows) the same as saying, "The more for me, the less for you." It is just the opposite. It would actually make more sense to say, "The more for me, the more for you, and the more for you, the less for me."

Discuss the conditions under which the conflict described in the above paragraph might be resolved by the mere clarification of your thinking on this topic.

Suggested Readings

Edward Bellamy, *Looking Backward* (Memorial Edition, 1917).
Fred Charles Iklé, *How Nations Negotiate* (1964).

John XXIII, *Pacem in Terris* (1963).
Immanuel Kant, *Perpetual Peace* (1796).
Paul Kecskemeti, *Strategic Surrender* (1964).
Arthur Lall, *Modern International Negotiation* (1966).
Kurt Lewin, *Resolving Social Conflicts* (Ch. 9, 1948).
John Locke, *Of Civil Government* (Second Essay, 1685).
Margaret Mead, *Cooperation and Conflict Among Primitive People* (1937).
Thomas More, *Utopia* (1516).
Philip Selznick, *TVA and the Grass Roots* (1949).
D. A. Strickland, "Ambiguity in Political Rhetoric," *Canadian Journal of Political Science,* Vol. 2, p. 338 (September 1969).
Thorstein Veblen, *The Nature of Peace* (1917).

CHAPTER 6

Opinion

An OPINION is whatever answer a person gives when asked what he thinks about particular things. A sneer or a smile is thus an opinion, if you know what question it refers to. Opinions are statements about the world, such as, "I would vote for Teddy Roosevelt any day." More generally, opinions are also feelings and attitudes toward ideas: "The less local government the better," "God bless the Flag," and so on. Opinions are not only indications of what a person thinks and wants at the moment; they are also indications of how he is likely to act in the future and how he wants you to act.

Public-opinion polls are useful insofar as they tell what people are likely to do and what they are likely to accept. In democratic political systems, leaders have to get reliable information about what people are going to do and what they will accept because the leader will be voted out of office if he gets out of touch with what the majority of the voters want. There are also people who want to know the opinions of others because they want to imitate them. If everybody had the same opinion on all issues, the political system would be quite predictable; it would also be quite weak because there would be fewer new ideas when new ideas were needed in emergencies or to solve new problems.

Opinions are of particular importance to a political system because the system cannot work if the leaders do not know what the followers are willing to do or if the followers do not know what the leaders want them to do. Many political conflicts begin because people have *misunderstood* what *other* people want, what *they* want, what is wanted *of* them, and what (if anything) will happen if they do not do what they are told to do by the authorities. For example, it has happened that a President appoints a Supreme Court Justice because he thinks he knows what the Justice's political opinions are; and then, after the Justice has his job for life, the President discovers that the Justice is deciding cases based on opinions that the President does not like.

Much confusion comes about because people fail to think about the difference between what they like and what they fear. People do what they like for no other reason than it is enjoyable or uplifting. There are other things they do out of fear (e.g., paying taxes if the only reason they pay them is fear of being forced to go to jail). Of course, there are people who claim, when forced to do something, that they wanted to do it all along. There are many, many people who have *lost track* of what they like as distinct from what others want them to like. And there are, of course, people (nearly everyone!) who discover that now they like things they used to be afraid of. Merriam was making a similar distinction when he said that the officials surround themselves with *miranda* (things to be admired) and *credenda* (things to be believed). The doctrines and the glitter of officialdom get all confused with people's fears and hopes; and many people end up either siding with functionaries because they are so impressed by them, or more or less openly resenting all authority because "nobody can make me do what I don't want to do."

Since opinions are indicators of what can and cannot be done in a political system, people often change their opinions so as to improve their chances of getting what they want. They may pretend that they agree with the majority in order to avoid being conspicious or that they agree with the winners in order to share in the benefits of winning (the "band-wagon effect"). They may deliberately say that they hold an opinion, when in fact they feel just the opposite, in order to get someone else to do something. For example, the Americans did not go to much trouble preparing to defend the fleet at Pearl Harbor because the Japanese *seemed* to be of the opinion that the best place to send their aircraft carriers was to the Gulf of Siam.

Thus, opinions become "moves" or weapons in political conflicts and conflict-resolutions. Since everyone knows this, a good deal of energy has to be expended to discover which opinions are pretenses and which are true. Sometimes you cannot discover this at all or not in time to make certain decisions. Decisions require information about what the alternatives really are. And the more misunderstanding and mis-information there is in the political system, the more decisions will be made that (a) will not work, (b) will make people do things they need not have done to satisfy the decision, and (c) will cost the decision-maker more than he need to have paid, e.g., by giving him new enemies or reducing the number of choices available to him in future decisions. When they fear that other people's opinions will make them look bad, people will try to keep those opinions from being voiced. Political authorities sometimes try to prevent opinions from being voiced because: (1) the opinions will damage their reputations; (2) the opinions will endanger the security of the country; (3) the opinions are untrue; (4) the opinions will provoke costly disputes and de-bates; or (5) the opinions will reveal new information, e.g., scientific discoveries, that leaves those particular political au-thorities with less power than they had before. Freedom of opinion also annoys leaders who have illusions about themselves or their countries and do not want anyone to laugh at their illusions.

People change their opinions as a result of *learning*. The simplest and most common kind of learning about the political system is learning who the officials are, what is going on from day to day, and what opinions will keep one out of trouble. The more general and very unusual learning about the political system is why it works the way it does, how to change it for the better, what it can and cannot do, and which opinions are most in tune with reality.

The word *policy* is used in this book from time to time. It means: (1) what the people who count *say* they are doing, (2) what they are *actually* doing, or (3) what they *intend* to do with the physical resources and people at their disposal. Some policies are intended to be *implemented* (the U.S. *is* building an interstate highway system); some are *symbolic* (the Russians say they are building a classless society when they probably are not); and some are *prophetic* (the policy of the U.S. is for full equality under the law, but it still has not gotten there).

Policy, then, can have several functions: to help all of the people, to help only some of the people, to hurt all of the people, or to hurt only some of the people. It can also be used to reassure the people that something useful and important is being done when in reality this is not true, and it can be used to persuade the people to support a certain set of politicians.

When it comes to policies that change things in a basic way, the results are revolutionary policies, as in Cuba under Castro. When it comes to stable societies, most policy follows Zipf's "principle of least effort"; that is, policies are made that introduce the least possible modification in the system.

Once set, policies can be hard to alter. After all, a politician who says one thing Monday and another thing Tuesday might be viewed as unprincipled or as all mixed-up. Consequently, many politicians are very vague about their policies. They might state that they want equal opportunity, but they will not say how to get it. Also, many politicians *say* they are pursuing an old and much-loved policy when they actually are doing something quite different. For example, it is not unknown for a politician to tell the people that he is seeking peace at the same time that he is preparing for war.

Socialization happens whenever a person learns something because someone else wants him to learn it. *Political socialization* happens whenever he learns something about politics in order to please someone else. Once in awhile, one can learn what he was not intended to learn.

Usually, political socialization is based on the idea that what *we* learn about politics is right and natural, and what some *other* people learn about politics is wrong and unnatural. Since the other people are learning what they think is natural, this can start all sorts of disagreements and even wars.

These kinds of fights are very hard to stop. People can feel strongly and be awfully sincere about their political beliefs. It is then difficult to convince them that what they believe to be true and obvious is not supported either by logic or by science. For example, when some people were taught that the Tsar was "the little father of Russia" and a marvellous man, and others were taught that he was an enemy of the people, they ended up fighting with each other.

Within a country, most people are taught the same things about politics. However, they are also taught different things. The similar things can lead to *consensus;* and the different things can lead to *conflict.* Consensus in the United States results when children are taught to respect the flag, the national heroes, the national anthem, and the Supreme Court. Conflict results when some are taught to be Democrats and others to be Republicans; when some are taught to like medicare and some that it is government "interference" with the doctors; when some are taught to respect the Supreme Court and some to scorn it.

Socialization of the intended sort does not always work. It fails when some people just will not accept what others are trying to teach them. This could be called political rebellion. Perhaps such rebels have been reading books that go against what their families, friends, and teachers have been telling them. Or they may encounter people who can explain the facts to them more satisfactorily. Or they may express certain opinions which they know will offend people with whom they are angry or toward whom they are resentful.

There are people who experience a very rapid change in their political views. This could be called a *political conversion.* Some people have believed in Communism for a long time, only to reject it suddenly and become angry anti-communists. A person may vote regularly for one party until an important person in his life dies, and he then begins to vote for another party. People sometimes support the government faithfully for years, then lose their jobs or their savings, and end up hating all politicians. In these cases, a painful event or an unstable personality may account for the conversion. One could call political conversion *socialization by events* because of the critical importance of a particular event, rather than a long process, in shaping political beliefs.

Most people, however, acquire their beliefs slowly over the years and do not change them. Most Democrats and Republicans in America will remain in the same party despite the speed at which the modern world is changing. People are no more apt to change their political views than they are apt to change their religious views.

As can readily be seen, the fact that some people change their minds about politics means that the political system as a whole will change. But the fact that most people will not change their minds about politics means that the political system as a whole will also tend not to change. This is one of the ways in which both stability and change are obtained in politics and society.

Perhaps you can now see why political socialization is so important to those people who want to keep the political system going as it is, or who want to correct what they think are its faults. To do this, children have to be taught to accept new or prevailing *opinions* or values. The best place to do this is in the family, where a lot of political socialization occurs. When children are taught to obey the policemen and the school teacher and to respect other children's playthings, they are being socialized in two very important values of our society— obedience to authority and respect for private property. When children are taught to work hard and get good grades, they are being socialized in the value of competition (some people claim that competition is the main value in America). When children are given a piggy bank in which to deposit their surplus pennies, they are being taught the values of thrift and accumulation.

All of these values have political meanings. For instance, the government could not borrow as much money as it does if other people were not busily saving it. And if people were not taught to be competitive, perhaps no one would want to be a U.S. Senator or a general.

Another important place where socialization occurs is in the schools. Civics courses, history courses, and patriotic exercises are supposed to build support for the political system. In fact, this is one of the important functions of the schools (see Structural-Functionalism in Chapter 2). In California, all college students must take a course in state government; the idea is that this will develop their loyalty to the State of California.

Socialization also takes place on the job. Medical doctors are taught to be against socialized medicine, while many blue-collar workers are taught to be for it. Socialization also occurs in the neighborhood, in fraternal, civic, and patriotic organizations, and among friends. *In fact, whenever people get together, they immediately begin to get socialized.*

Mortification is another form of socialization. It can be quite dramatic. It is done to show an individual that he is not at all like he was before. Mortification involves the physical or psychological debasement of a person. Examples would be the shaving of the head of an army recruit—this symbolizes that he is no longer a civilian. Prisons, which are also political institutions, use mortification for much the same reason—to show that the individual is no longer a citizen. This may be done by fastening a ball and chain to the prisoner, assigning him a ludicrous uniform, or by tattooing a number on his forehead.

An interesting form of socialization is *apprenticeship.* This means that a person learns things by observing and following an admired person or model. It is said that Prime Minister Wilson of Great Britain learned how to act in a public forum by imitating President Kennedy. People often follow the behavior styles of their leaders so that they will know how to act if they should themselves become leaders.

Training is still another way of socializing people. Schools train people for citizenship; military academies train people for the armed forces; Junior Achievement trains people for the economy; Komsomols train people for positions in the Soviet political system. Associations like these try to socialize people *before* they become members, so that after they become members the association will not have to spend so much time and money teaching them how to act and what to believe, or to try to show them how marvelous it will be to finally join a particular association.

Excommunications are also intended to socialize. To "make an example" of someone is supposed to teach others not to behave the way "someone" did. Trotsky was excommunicated from Russia and the Communist Party to teach others not to follow his beliefs. Sometimes leaders try to "read out" other people from an association, say from the Democratic or Republican parties, by disavowing their support. Armies may strip an offender of his military insignia in a public ceremony before expelling him from the association. Associations that emphasize ideological purity and consistency use excommunications more frequently than do other forms of associations.

Rites of passage are socializing events, too. An oath, a baptism, a confirmation, an inaugural parade, the issuance of a uniform or a membership card, learning a secret handshake, are all intended to show a person that he should act differently than before, at least in some circumstances.

Whoever can get others to adopt an opinion is a LEADER. That is the same as saying that a leader is someone whom others will obey—because some of the opinions have to do with how one acts in the real world. And if the followers do not follow through with the action, they have not really "adopted" the leader's opinions.

This definition holds even where the leader first goes around and finds out what the followers want and then announces that he wants exactly what they want. In such a case, it is said that a person is a spokesman for others. But even a spokesman is a leader if people pretend he is (see W. I. Thomas' law, p. 102) and if he changes or adds to the opinions of his followers.

Sometimes leaders merely hold opinions which are the average of the opinions of the followers. They occupy a middle-ground among the opinions of the followers. We call such leaders "brokers" because they are making deals and trades between followers who want inconsistent things.

Other leaders hold opinions that are somewhat more extreme than those of the followers. This is certainly the image that comes to mind when one says that some people "lead" (i.e., are ahead of) and others "follow" (i.e., are behind).

It should be clear now that leaders need something from

their followers. Whatever that is (money, votes, fear, deference, love, or prayers), it is called SUPPORT. Followers support leaders in different ways, on different issues, and at different intensities. When it happens that a leader does not have very strong support, he is able to get less done in the political system, especially in a genuinely democratic system.

The leader gives the followers something, too. One can loosely call these things the rewards or "payoffs" of obedience. They consist of money, offices, honors, policies wanted by the followers, feelings of strength and security, admiration at the skill and importance of "our leader."

You may notice that we tend to speak of *the* leader. It cannot be denied that there are groups and organizations in which there are several leaders. Julius Caesar himself was for a while a part of a three-man team, the triumvirate. It did not last. Human beings have a strong tendency to want to know who is *really* the boss. This is because so many people do not want to take charge of *themselves.* They want to pretend that there is some one person, somewhere in the government, who can be blamed for all the hardships of life. (It is more dramatic that way!) It is also because people tend to search high and low for heroes. The interesting thing about heroes, and villains, is that even though they are the strongest guys around, each has his secret weakness (think of Achilles, Sampson, or Rumpel-stiltzkin). Hence, one can fear and admire his political heroes and still feel smug.

Leaders and heroes play an important part in the secret belief of many people that someone has to arrive on the scene and rescue them all from their current problems. Whether it is to be Napoleon or the Lord Buddha, he will cast the Wicked from the Temple and, with a wave of the magic wand, straighten everything out for good. That way it is not necessary for them to work hard and find their own sensible solutions to the problems. (This belief is like the belief some women have that a Dark Stranger will come and abduct them. It is also like the belief that so many people have that they are Cinderellas and may some day awaken to find that they are Kings, or Queens, or both.)

Whoever ends up being the leaders in a political system are called the ELITE (i.e., the chosen ones). All others are referred to as the MASS. In most modern societies, leaders in one sort of activity are not the same people as the leaders in another area. So one can speak about "the political elite" or "the industrial elite" or "the military elite."

In normal times, these specialized elites have more influence in their areas than anyone else in the system (this statement can be used as another definition of elite). It is not surprising, therefore, to discover that the elites usually know more about what is going on in their special areas. If a person can find out who is getting the most information and whose opinions are most widely publicized, he has probably located the elite. Some of the information given out by the elites is called PROPAGANDA, which means that some facts have been left out or twisted in an effort to get certain opinions accepted.

Political skills are like other skills or abilities in that they involve the manipulation of the material, social, and symbolic environment. One thinks of a skillful politician as one who knows how to use physical things (television, airplanes, defense contracts) to his best advantage. He is also one who knows how to use people to help him in office—he might cajole, entice, threaten, plead, or force them to help him. But his skill at *mass propaganda,* or symbol-manipulation, can be even more important. *Knowing which words and gestures will get what responses is the essence of propaganda.* Propaganda differs from socialization in that propaganda refers to the activity of the propagandist while socialization refers to, among other things, the *effect* of propaganda on people.

One kind of propaganda is the *complexity* argument. For example, it sometimes consists in bombarding people with words about gross national product, unemployment rates, inventories, and tax schedules. Since the politicians know that very few people can understand these things *in the form they are presented,* the people will tend to let the politicians have their own way. Thus, the technique here is to make the people believe that things are so complex that only the politicians, the experts, and the professionals should decide. Or, in foreign affairs, politicians can disarm their critics by the complexity argument. If their opponents are poets, farmers, or businessmen, what can they possibly know about international affairs which, say some politicians, are inordinately complex! This can be a very effective way of making people shut-up.

Another effective device is the *simplicity* technique which is just the opposite of the complexity method of propaganda. This method is based on over-simplifying things and playing on people's needs for quick, easy explanations. The U.S.S.R. talks about capitalist foreign policy, ignoring the fact that France and the U.S. follow different policies even though they are both capitalist countries. Some politicians talk about the Free World, even though parts of it, like Haiti, are not free at all. Or politicians may offer an easy end to racial disorder (e.g., a get-tough policy) if people will just elect them to office, even when it really is clear that there is no easy solution.

Another ingredient in propaganda is the promise of a glowing future. People are so hungry for such promises that it is hard to tell whether the exaggerations originate more with the maker or with the recipient of the promise. Thus, when Jehovah promised to lead His people to a land "flowing with milk and honey" (*Exodus*, 3:8), Moses probably understood this to be a figure of speech. Immigrants coming to America, however, sometimes act as though they secretly believed that maybe some of the streets, or at least side streets, *are* paved with gold. And when Hitler promised the Germans a very unlikely thing—an empire that would last 1000 years—most of them evidently believed him or wanted to.

Virtually all politicians also use sacred words to get things their own way—words like "free enterprise," "human dignity," "peace in our time," or "the war to end wars." They use these even when they (1) do not believe them or (2) do not know what they mean, if anything.

Part and parcel of most of these techniques is the skillful use of emotions. Throughout history, politicians have tried to stir up the people by playing on their emotions, prejudices, biases, and fears. This was Hitler's main method. One other thing: not only politicians use propaganda, although they are very fond of it. *Anyone who tries to convince someone else about anything political is probably a political propagandist.* Everybody wants his opinions taken seriously.

Over the centuries, the opinions of certain people have

been taken so seriously that these became *laws*. In the Bible, a set of basic laws, the Ten Commandments, was given to Moses by God. In modern political systems, representatives make laws in legislatures, or the political elite announces new laws in the name of the people. A LAW is an opinion that most of the people in a political system will adopt *and* which certain specialized officials will enforce by injuring the ones who will not adopt it.

When someone speaks favorably of law—as in praise of "law and order" or of "the rule of law"—they mean that it is a good thing to live in a political system that is predictable and tells them where to stand. The opposite would be a country in which the leaders are frequently changing things around so that people can never be sure that they might not be punished for offending the private feelings of some official.

Even political systems that are not strong on law and order have some kinds of laws or rules. One should not forget that a very orderly system (in addition to being unbearably dull) can be undesirable from the standpoint of the people who are not getting what they want from it. Hence, one hears people say of such a system: "*Whose* law and *whose* order?"

A definition of *political system* might be that it is those people who obey the same laws. By this definition, there can be several political systems in the same country: the people in New York do not obey the same laws as those in Alabama; criminals have a different set of rules than citizens do; certain religious groups have additional laws they follow; and so on.

Law and order have been the main values of many political systems. Two other basic values that are often discussed are *property* and *liberty*. Many political theories begin with statements concerning property. Human beings are, as St. Thomas Aquinas remarked, necessitous creatures; and we fall to fighting over things, edible and non-edible. These conflicts are due to basic human needs (food, shelter, companionship, and the like) or to greed. The conflicts themselves are so entertaining to bystanders that some political systems pretend it is *virtuous* to fight about property, long after the contestants have enough for their basic needs.

Trouble is what politics is all about. Conflicts over the ownership of property can be *controlled* to some extent if there are laws that help define who the "real" owner is. By permitting people to fight, instead, about what the *law* really means and by encouraging them at the same time to try to get their property away from one another, some political systems keep up everyone's interest without letting things get out of hand.

Liberty (or freedom) is an impulse in another direction. It means that whatever was the nature of the laws and of property *before,* people *now* want to be free of them. The question is, freedom *from* what or *for* what? That part of the battle-cry is usually left out. What it comes down to most of the time is "freedom from the oppressors." Since, as shown earlier, different people have different opinions as to who the oppressors are,[1] you rarely meet anyone who does not share a good opinion of freedom.

Sample Theorem

Where people know or believe that serious conflicts are possible within their political system, they will want the political opinions of others to be in conformity with their own.

Proof

(i) When one person tells another his wants, that is an expression of opinions (*Ex def.*).

(ii) There is always some risk that a person will be misunderstood, that what he really means will not be stated clearly or heard correctly (Assumption 2).

(iii) Whenever an opinion is misunderstood, there is some risk that the hearer will believe it to be the statement of a want inconsistent with his own wants (Assumption 3).

(iv) A conflict is the result when people want the same thing or inconsistent things (*Ex def.*).

---

[1] Favorites over the years have been: kings, priests, intellectuals, the British Foreign Office, International Jewry, dictators, industrialists, the ignorant masses, Popery, Wall Street, "the interests," aristocrats, the idle rich, landlords, Islam, the Masons, militarists, anarchists, socialists, Protestants, foreign devils, "wasps" blacks, imperialists, democrats, Reds, and Satan.

(v) People avoid conflicts unless they believe the conflict will benefit them (Assumption 1).

(vi) In all conflicts, there is some risk that the outcome will be that some persons will not get what they want (*Ex def.*).

(vii) If an opinion is stated, there is, therefore, *some risk* that it will be the expression of a want, and that the want will bring about a conflict, and the conflict will result in something people do not want.

(viii) And thus, if the opinion does not get stated, there is less risk that such a conflict will arise.

(ix) And hence, people will want conformity of opinions when they fear that the statement of new opinions may lead to serious conflicts.

Problems

1. If there were a political system in which a third of the people want to declare war on a neighboring country, a fourth of the people do not want to declare war, and the rest have no opinion on the question, what is the democratic solution in such a case?

2. In one of his essays, Henry David Thoreau said that the majority should vote on an issue only if they were indifferent to it. Assume that he is right and that the American public is divided on the issue of socialized medicine (sometime in the future) as follows: 23 per cent for, 27 per cent against, 50 per cent "no opinion." What would be the democratic solution in this case?

3. In Joseph Heller's famous novel, *Catch 22,* an American airman and an old Italian are talking politics in Rome during the American occupation of Italy in World War II. How would you analyze the following passages, using the above analysis of opinion?

[AIRMAN] . . . Italy was occupied by the Germans and is now being occupied by us. You don't call that doing very well do you?
[OLD MAN] But of course I do. The Germans are being driven out, and we are still here. In a few years you will be gone, too, and we will still be

here. . . . Italian soldiers are not dying any more. But American and German soldiers are. I call that doing extremely well. . . .
[AIRMAN] . . . I really don't understand what you're saying. You talk like a madman.
[OLD MAN] But I live like a sane one. I was a fascist when Mussolini was on top, and I am anti-fascist now that he has been deposed. I was fanatically pro-German when the Germans were here to protect us against the Americans, and now that the Americans are here . . . I am fanatically pro-American. . . .
[AIRMAN] But you're a turncoat! A time-server! A shameful, unscrupulous opportunist!
[OLD MAN] I am a hundred and seven years old.
[AIRMAN] Anything worth living for is worth dying for.
[OLD MAN] And anything worth dying for is certainly worth living for.

4. Politicians who want to stay in office are usually interested in knowing what the public thinks about the issues of the day. If a politician fails to understand what the public thinks, he may lose the next election to a politician who does know. Therefore, politicians (and social scientists) have invented all sorts of ways of finding out about public opinion. Politicians read newspapers and magazines, maintain a large correspondence with the "people back home," talk to "average" people, and conduct public-opinion *polls* to find out how the people feel about political problems.

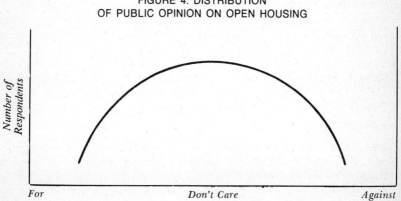

FIGURE 4. DISTRIBUTION
OF PUBLIC OPINION ON OPEN HOUSING

Number of Respondents

For   *Don't Care*   *Against*

FIGURE 5. DISTRIBUTION
OF PUBLIC OPINION ON OPEN HOUSING

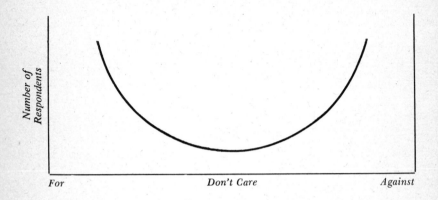

Suppose that a certain politician had a poll taken which showed that some people were very, very concerned about a certain issue, for example, whether or not Negroes should be free to live wherever they can afford to live. This issue is so important that any politician who went against the people would be sure to lose the next election. Suppose further that this "open housing" issue was one which produced the *distribution* of

FIGURE 6. DISTRIBUTION
OF PUBLIC OPINION ON OPEN HOUSING

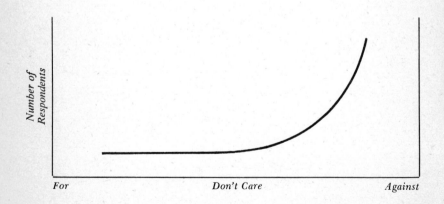

opinions presented in Figure 4. What do you think the politician would do about open housing in this case?

Suppose, however, that public opinion was distributed in another way on the same issue, as shown in Figure 5. Now how do you think the politicians would behave?

How would the politician respond if the polls showed that opinion was distributed as indicated in Figure 6?

5. People may have three kinds of political opinions, and these three kinds of opinions may be combined and distributed in any number of ways. One kind of opinion is *cognitive:* "The Democrats (Republicans) control the state Senate." Some opinions are *evaluative,* or estimates of the consequences of a fact (or what is believed to be a fact): "Since the Democrats (Republicans) control the state Senate, we can (cannot) expect a right-to-work law." Finally, some opinions are *affective* and thus express emotional or value-laden reactions to existing or possible cognitive and evaluative states of mind: thus, "The Democrats (Republicans) control the state Senate (cognitive opinion); we can therefore be sure that they will (will not) pass a right-to-work law (evaluative opinion); and one thing I dislike (like) intensely is right-to-work laws" (affective opinion). Now assume that the politicians had taken a poll and discovered the following about the electorate's opinions. How would the *politicians'* opinions be affected by the data?

OPINION DISTRIBUTION	
Cognitive	
Proportion of electorate knowing which party controls state Senate	51%
Evaluative	
Proportion of electorate which knows which party controls the Senate also believes a right-to-work law probable	25%
Affective	
Proportion of electorate thinking a right-to-work law likely is very much in favor of the law	15%

6. Consider the following lines from a play (*The Fall of the City*) by Archibald MacLeish. Why, in your opinion, might people want, or want to believe in, such a leader?

The Voices of Citizens

The city is doomed!
  There is no holding it!

Let the conqueror have it! It's his!

. . . .

Men must be ruled!

Fools must be mastered!

Rigor and fast
Will restore us our dignity!

Chains will be liberty!

. . . .

The Voice of the Announcer

. . . .

Yes! . . .
He's there in the end of the street in the
  shadow. We see him!
He looks huge—a head taller than anyone:
Broad as a brass door: a hard hero:
Heavy heel on the brick: clanking with
  metal:

. . . .

He mounts by the pyramid—stamps on the
  stairway—turns—
His arm rises—his visor is opening . . .
(There is an instant' breathless silence:
then the voice of the Announcer low—
almost a whisper).
        There's no one! . . .
There' no one at all! . . .
        No one! . . .
        The helmet is hollow!

. . . .

Listen! They're shouting like the troops in a
  victory. Listen—

'The city of masterless men has found a
master!'
You'd say it was they were the conquerors:
that they had conquered.[2]

7. If you were writing propaganda for the Opposition Party, what might you make of the following facts? Your country was attacked and had to give up many of its colonies because most of its fleet was destroyed during a surprise attack on a certain harbor. The Ruling Party had control of your government's vast espionage and intelligence organization, with agents and informants all over the world. This organization had reports, some days in advance of the surprise attack, that the harbor would be attacked. The leaders of the Ruling Party did very little to prepare for such an attack. Instead they believed that an attack by the same enemy was going to be made elsewhere in the world. The military experts at the time mostly agreed that the attack would probably be elsewhere. The intelligence reports indicated that attacks might be made in dozens and dozens of places—in far more places, in fact, than the enemy could possibly have intended. Furthermore, so many messages were coming in about the enemy's plans that the intelligence agency could not keep track of them all.

8. Consider Rappaport's law: "The more churches, the more taverns." How would you apply this to political ideologies? Incidentally, where do you assume attitudes and beliefs come from?

Suggested Readings

Ruth Benedict, *Patterns of Culture* (1934).
Kenneth E. Boudling, *Image: Knowledge in Life and Society* (1956).
Angus Campbell, P. Converse, W. Miller, and D. Stokes, *The American Voter* (1969).
R. Dawson and K. Prewitt, *Political Socialization* (1969).
Karl Deutsch, *The Nerves of Government* (1963).

[2]Reprinted from *The Fall of the City* by Archibald MacLeish, © 1937 and 1965, by permission of Houghton Mifflin Company.

Murray Edelman, *The Symbolic Uses of Politics* (1964).

Erich Fromm, *Escape from Freedom* (1941).

Herbert Hyman, *Political Socialization* (1959).

Stanley Kelley, *Professional Public Relations and Political Power* (1956).

V. O. Key, Jr., *Public Opinion and Democracy* (1961).

Clyde Kluckhohn, *Mirror for Man* (1949).

Robert Lane and David Sears, *Public Opinion* (1964).

Harold D. Lasswell, *Psychopathology and Politics* (1931).

Seymour M. Lipset, *Political Man* (1956).

Norman Luttbeg, ed., *Public Opinion and Public Policy* (1968).

Charles Merriam, *Political Power* (1934).

D. A. Strickland and R. E. Johnston, "Issue Elasticity in Political Systems," *Journal of Political Economy,* Vol. 78, p. 1069, (October 1970).

Roberta Wohlstetter, *Pearl Harbor* (1962).

H. Zipf, *Human Behavior and the Principle of Least Effort* (1949).

CHAPTER 7

Agency

AGENCY is one person's letting another person speak for him on some topic. A salesman is an agent of the company he works for because he is authorized to make sales in the name of the company. A legislator is an agent of the people he represents, or at least of the ones who voted for him. A delegate is an agent for those who sent him to the meeting; he speaks on their behalf only on matters specified by them.

A *general agent* is an agent who speaks for someone (called the PRINCIPAL) on *any* subject on which the principal is capable of acting. Clearly, there are no general agents in a political system because: (1) there are too many opinions and preferences for any one agent (representative) to be able to promote all of them at once; (2) some of the opinions are inconsistent with others, and thus it would be logically impossible to represent them all at the same time; (3) the opinions are changing all the time; (4) on some (so-called "private") subjects, the people never intended to let the representative speak for them.

(A parent is a general agent for a small child, but for the

very reason that the child is not yet able *even* to decide which things to do for itself and which to delegate to agents. There may be political systems in which the leader-follower relation is more like parent-child than agent-principal.)

Though it is impossible to be a general agent for another adult in reality, people try to do it for two reasons: (1) So-called ambitious people sometimes feel that they are *closer* to achieving their ambitions when they have lots of followers, constituents, supporters, slaves, and the like. (2) People who do not like to answer for their own decisions may want to pretend that someone else (the scapegoat) is responsible when things go wrong. When things go right, they want to believe that the other fellow could not have done it without their vote. The general-agent type of leader therefore becomes either a hero or a devil, or both, as the occasion requires. The advantage of this technique is that a person can have the illusion that his political opinions are never wrong. The disadvantage is that one has to find someone who is willing to pretend that he is responsible for the principal's opinions *as well as* for whatever happens in the world of events.

A leader also functions as the *memory* (superior knowledge and experience) of the group. This is why powerful positions in political systems are so often occupied by older members.

When leaders get to be heroes, they belong to the category of what used to be known as *idols.* Individuals are only one object of idolization; men also idolize things like Golden Calves, Money, Freedom, America the Beautiful, the People, Progress, Harvard, and so on. When one likes an idol, he refers to it as a value or belief or conviction. When he does not like it, he refers to it as idolatry or fanaticism or paganism.

Idols are agents. They are physical and symbolical representatives of the things men especially like about themselves. Thus, if a person is proud of being a Hindu, a German, or an Eskimo, that means, in a manner of speaking, that he has *generalized* on the things he likes about himself and has *attributed* them to a large number of people who are "just like" him. Whereas statistics merely provide ways of describing the frequency with which certain things appear in the natural world, agency permits things that are *wanted* and *wished for* to be attributed to large parts of the world, whether they exist there or not.

Furthermore, agency is a type of *specialization*. For instance, we can all sing; but we tend to believe that only professional singers can "really" sing. We do this even to the point of *forgetting* that Caruso, Leontyne Price, and the Beatles are by all accounts human beings like us. In this way our singing idols become agents; they sing *for* us and not just *to* us.

Once the original connection between people and their idols has been forgotten, the idols appear to be far more intimidating, and, at the same time, dealings with them become confused. In politics, this gives rise to the problem of *loyalty*. Loyalty is a problem because some people get scared when they notice that they and their friends have forgotten all about the idols or have ceased to like them. Then the forgetful ones are denounced for being selfish, traitorous, ungrateful, criminal, or otherwise disloyal. The problem of loyalty is a very severe one for some people because: (1) when they first agreed to like the idol, they invested a lot of their self-esteem in it; and (2) when it is forgotten or rejected they feel belittled, or (3) they cannot admit it was a mistake to begin with (for fear that the admission implies their self-esteem was not worth much in the first place). Once a person feels strongly about being a citizen of Andorra, therefore, he finds it awfully embarrassing to be accused of any disloyalty to that Republic.

For other people, the idol is even more important as an agent that has captured *so much* of their self-esteem that there is not any left. Agents of this sort are seen as *rescuers,* and the person feels so desperately low and empty that he believes he will never survive unless the King, President de Gaulle, Chairman Mao, or Mother Russia will look after him. Hence, one can run into people on buses or in bars or subways who are muttering angrily about sending the Swedes back to where they came from or muttering happily about the wonders of the Irish: hating the one group or loving the other helps such people feel that they count for something and that somebody (the fellow idolizer) likes them despite it all.

In democracies, most people vote for a leader on the basis of the *probability* that he will do what they would do if *they* were running the political system. In systems where the leader has to get a majority of the votes to win office, it is very hard to determine the probabilities because the leader is saying ambiguous things in order to please as many people as possible. In such a case, people become especially interested in the personality and character of the leader, as a key to what he is likely to do in the future.

Even when the leader is very clear about what he intends to do and about what the others expect of him, he has two problems: (1) He is the agent of so *many* different people, with so many opinions, and with different feelings of *urgency* about different opinions, that he cannot do *anything* without frustrating some of his constituents. (2) Times change, and the leader often has to act on new issues about which he has never asked his constituents' opinions. If he has time to ask their opinions before acting he usually does not have time or money to ask *everybody's* opinion. The shortness of time and money is the reason that *ideology* (i.e., general ideas about the future of the political system), like personality and character, is important in choosing an agent—it gives a clue as to how he is *likely* to act in situations that have not come up yet.

A political system in which one person is supposed to be the agent of everybody else in the country is called an *autocracy* or a *monarchy*. A political system in which a few people are supposed to represent everybody else is called an *oligarchy* or *aristocracy*. Where a minority is supposed to accept people chosen by the majority as their agents, it is called a *democracy*. Where no one is supposed to represent anybody else, it is called *anarchy*.

CONSULTATION is (1) A, who is B's agent, talking to B to make sure he knows what B really wants on some particular subject, or (2) A, though not B's agent, asking B's advice or opinion on some particular subject. Consultation usually refers to *representatives,* who are supposed to know the wants of the people they represent (their constituents), or to *rulers,* who may want to know what people will and will not accept. In a political system where the rulers are elected and are responsible to those who elect them, the rulers are also representatives—so one would expect to find more consultation there than in other kinds of political systems. Where the wants of people in the system are

FIGURE 7. SYSTEM A

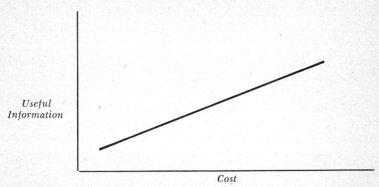

The more spent to get useful information, the more such information acquired (proportionately). (A curve inclined in just the opposite direction would be unrealistic. Why?)

FIGURE 8. SYSTEM B

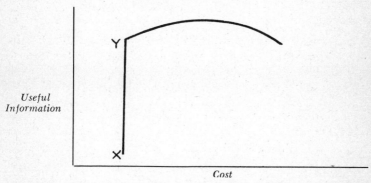

Up to some (optimum) point, the more spent on information, the more useful information acquired, and beyond that point the money is being wasted. There may be some "free information" in the above graph, the area between point x and point y—which is simply given to the political leader without any expenditure of time, money, or effort on his part. Information which he would acquire in his normal life, without any additional expenditure might also be thought of as free information. (If the curve were turned upside down, then it would be the most economical to spend either very little or a lot on information. Something in between might yield, for example, such a mixture of true and false information that the leader could not use any of it because he could not tell which items were true.)

FIGURE 9. SYSTEM C

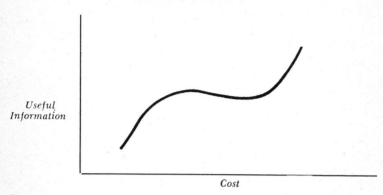

Useful
Information

Cost

There is a range in the middle of this curve where increasing expenditures on information is a waste of money; except for that range, this is like System A. (If this curve were inclined in the opposite direction, it too would be unrealistic. Why?)

incompatible, where there have been violent conflicts, or where the rulers believe that they already know what the others think, one would expect to find relatively little consultation.

Of course, consultation requires time and money. Whether it is worthwhile depends on the value of the new information to the people involved, compared with the cost of getting it (including the risk of provoking people on subjects thet would not otherwise be thinking about). The relationships between these factors might (in defferent political systems) look like those presented in Figures 7, 8, and 9.

Sample Theorem

Political representatives speak with the power of all the people they represent.

Proof

(i) It is possible to change one's opinions, to compromise one's wants, and to capitulate (Assumptions 4 and 7).

(ii) By voting for a representative, people accept the opinions he represents as the best available alternatives; that is, they abandon some of their own wants on the grounds that what the candidate represents is the best they can get for the time being (*Ex def.* Decision).

(iii) Those who did not vote for the representative are, during his term of office, either represented by him or by no one.

(iv) If they do not take the opportunity to express the opinion that he does *not* represent their opinions on particular issues, they give the impression that he *does* (*Ex def.* Decision; Thoreau's maxim).

(v) That is, the representative speaks for all the people who actively or passively give other people the impression that he speaks for them (*Ex def.* Agency and Opinion).

(vi) Hence, when the representative speaks, it can be assumed that he speaks with the force of all the people in his district excepting those who have declared that he does not represent them.

Sample Theorem

Political representatives can speak for certain only for themselves.

Proof

(i) People not only have different wants and opinions, but their wants and opinions change at different times for different reasons (Assumption 3).

(ii) Thus, the more people in a political unit, the more their wants and opinions are differentiated and are changing (*Ex def.*).

(iii) With regard to any particular person, his opinions *may* be different at this instant from what they were the previous instant (Step i).

(iv) Hence, at any given instant a political representative can only be sure of his own opinion and can only be sure he is speaking for himself.

Problems

1. Consider the following situation: Senator X was elected with a majority of 150,000 votes, or 52 per cent of the votes cast for that office in that election. During the first year of his term he has changed his mind and no longer supports the War on Poverty. Public opinion polls show that over 60 per cent of the eligible voters in his state strongly support the War on Poverty. An attempt was made to recall him, but it failed. He has four and one-half years before he comes up for election again. Analyze this situation, using the concepts presented in this chapter.

2. There have been elections in this country in which the President received less than 50 per cent of the votes cast for that office but more than any opponent, and was declared elected. In what sense would a President elected in that way be the agent of all the people?

3. Considering that a Senator is elected by a majority of those voting in his state, and that legislation passes the Senate whenever a majority of the Senators will vote for it, and that some Senators have more influence in the Senate than others— would you say that the Senate is an oligarchic or a democratic body? Why?

4. Assume that you are a Congressman from a district which is changing rapidly: in the last few years 55 per cent of the White-Anglo-Saxon-Protestant ("wasp") population has moved to other neighborhoods; some of the newcomers are Puerto Ricans and some are poor "wasps" from the southern Appalachians; there have been more crimes of violence in the district in the last year than in the previous five years; landlords have complained to you that their buildings are being "broken to pieces" and parents have complained to you that their children are not safe going to and from school. What would you do to help prevent this situation from getting worse?

5. Suppose you were a Senator from a state where the Americans for Democratic Action were quite influential, and you wanted to know what stand the organization would take on

Federal Aid to Education. Suppose further that the national chairman of the ADA tells you one thing and the leaders of your state ADA chapter tell you something else. How would you go about discovering the real position of the ADA on this issue?

6. What if you lived in a region of the state where most of the people are farmers and none of the towns is very large. Moreover, what if the people in the big cities of your state did not have as much voting power as the people in your region— for example, the seats in the state legislature might be divided up so that the 100,000 people in your region got to choose one representative, while in the big cities there was only one representative for 500,000 people. Let's assume that the city folks were going to the U.S. Supreme Court to argue that in a democracy everybody's vote should count the same and the Legislature should be re-divided. (a) What arguments would you make on behalf of the people from your region? (b) What, if anything, would happen to your region if you lost? (*Reynolds* v. *Sims,* 377 U.S. 533 [1964].)

7. Occasionally, voters in the United States get very angry because a Senator or Congressman goes ahead and does what *he* thinks is right even though he knows that the people who put him in office want him to do something else. There are now ways (e.g., the recall, initiative, referendum, and impeachment) in some political systems to force leaders to do what the voters want, or at least to prevent them from doing what the voters *do not* want. If you were trying to defend a leader who was defying public opinion in this way, what points might you mention? (see Edmund Burke's "Letter to the Bristol Sheriffs.")

8. Iceland is the oldest still-existing democracy. Why do you suppose this is so?

Suggested Readings

Robert Agger, D. Goldrich, B. Swanson, *The Rulers and the Ruled* (1964).
Francis Bacon, *Novum Organum* (Chs. 39–68, 1620).
Robert Dahl, *Who Governs?* (1961).
Alexander George and Juliette George, *Woodrow Wilson and Colonel House* (1956).

Floyd Hunter, *Top Leadership, U.S.A.* (1959).
Henry Kariel, *In Search of Authority* (1964).
Alexander Leighton, *The Governing of Men* (1945).
Donald Matthews, *The Social Background of Political Decision-Makers* (1954).
Lester Milbrath, *Political Participation* (1965).
John Stuart Mill, *Considerations on Representative Government* (1861).
Otto Rank, *The Myth of the Birth of the Hero* (1935).

CHAPTER **8**

Association

It is true that people who have anything at all to do with one another are *associated*. However, when one speaks of an ASSOCI-ATION, he usually means people who are deliberately cooperating for some reason(s). To cooperate means to develop some rules (norms, laws) which the people in the association will follow or say they will follow. To make an association is, therefore, a political act, because it means getting people to do what they did not previously want to do (see Chapter 2).

There are many, many kinds of associations in modern societies—churches, gangs, business, corporations, families, card clubs, veterans' groups, friendships, mobs, fraternities, and so on. Not all associations are political associations, however.

What is usually meant by a POLITICAL ASSOCIATION is one made up of people who want to get large numbers of people to do things they otherwise would not do. Thus, a police department is a political association because policemen generally try to make people obey the laws; a court is a political association for the same reason; and a religious movement is a political association to the extent that it changes the behavior of numerous people (e.g., by persuading them not to participate in the political system or by making them agitate for laws that protect the religion). The "associated" people need not be in the same place. They may share the same beliefs, and they may or may not be in communication. Thus, Canadians who want *Quebec libre* are expressing attitudes which they believe they share with people in France.

It should be noted that countries vary a good deal in the kind of associations they have and permit. The more industrialized countries tend to have a greater variety (even though they do not all permit their citizens to organize political groups and political parties freely). The less industrialized, so-called traditional, societies are more apt to have fewer associations and associations which (like family and class) one belongs to by birth rather than by joining. Just as a white person cannot join the Black Power movement in America, so a farmer cannot join the aristocracy in Ethiopia.

There are many kinds of political associations. They include: (1) *political parties* which usually are made up of people who want to change certain things about the whole country by getting their agents into office; (2) *regimes* which is what political parties are called when they are running the government; (3) *pressure groups* which are made up of people who (compared to political parties) are interested only in a few topics and do not offer to run the government themselves; (4) *factions* which are made up of people who disagree partly with the others in the association they belong to, for example, the Buddhists in South Vietnam; and (5) *cliques* which are very small groups made up of friends who believe that their own wants are almost identical with one another, though different in many ways from those of the other people in the faction or association. The government itself is such as association, and rapidly growing. (For example, the number of officers in the Canadian Department of External Affairs increased from 18 in 1930 to 705 in 1967.)

ENTROPY in a political system refers to the degree of non-cooperation between the people in the system. Whether the people cooperate because they want to or because they are forced to, the more association there is the less entropy there is.

That is to say, *high entropy* means that the people in the system have different wants and are going off in different directions; they are *not* coordinating their behaviors. *Low entropy* means that the people in the system have concentrated their efforts and are more in agreement about what to do.

When A can do something which B cannot do, the difference between A and B is called POWER. Sometimes A can do it because A himself has some quality (skill, physical attributes, persistence, and the like), and sometimes A can do it because he has an opportunity that B does not have (e.g., A is lucky, has connections, lives on the right side of the tracks, and so forth). Usually it is a little of both.

If A and B have conflicting wants and if A can get what he wants (i.e., A wins) and B therefore cannot get what he wants (i.e., B loses), then A has POLITICAL POWER. The influential are those who get the most of what there is to get. (Lasswell, *Politics: Who Gets What, When, and How.)* That is, political power *not only* tells "who gets what, when, and how" (as Professor Harold Lasswell said), but it also tells *at the same time* who *loses* what, when, and how.

When a person says A has political power because of some skill, he is really saying that in a political system certain skills are valued more than others—which is equal to saying that the values and valued qualities of individuals vary from system to system. In America, men are viewed as important and powerful if they have some of the following qualities: a large bank account, good looks and correct weight, oratorical skills, knowledge of the market place and how to make money, knowledge of the political market place and how to make power, and so on. These men become important not so much because *they* value these qualities, but because *other people* value these qualities. An individual with great oratorical skill, a huge bank account, and control over political office may be ranked very low on his own or someone else's scale of values.

People are mainly interested in what *will become of themselves,* their ambitions, their fortunes, their freedom, their friends and family. Hence, people always try to guess ways in which to maintain or increase their own political power in the future. *If* they are convinced that A will win the next conflict, it is cheaper for everyone to give in to A without actually going through with the conflict. When that happens, A is said to have PERCEIVED POLITICAL POWER; that is, people *act* as if A had the power, even though he might not have the power if they went to the trouble of carrying through the conflict. For example, people in a country may treat the Prime Minister as though he has lots of power even when public opinion is against him and he probably would lose office if there were an election that day.

Many political troubles are important—despite the fact that they appear to be quite trivial and silly—because they are *tests* of the direction in which political power is changing. If A loses these little tests, he is less likely to go to the trouble of entering into a full-fledged conflict with B at a later time. For instance, if the tests seem to show that A will not be able to prevent his powerful ally C from also becoming the ally of his (A's) enemy B, then it may be a good idea for A to avoid future conflicts with B.

Now it will be clear why people enter political associations. They thereby increase, or believe they will increase, their individual political power. If 10,000 people agree to vote against a certain politician, or to pool their money for some purpose, or to try to change public policy through pressure tactics, they will probably have more success than if each of them worked on his own. The advantages of forming associations are, of course, watered down if other people form other associations to do just the opposite thing. This often happens. For example, labor unions and management groups counteract one another; and pacifist groups may find themselves competing with pro-war groups. When this happens, the political conflicts may appear to be going on between private groups, with the governmental authorities acting as mediators or judges.

Another thing that can happen is that the people who form an association end up fighting among themselves. The leaders may disagree with the followers; the group may split up; rival leaders may argue for somewhat different goals; members may disagree over tactics, time-tables, personalities, and so on. When these things happen (as they always do in some measure), the association has less political power than it otherwise would have had.

As seen in the discussion of conflict (Chapter 4), people often get into conflicts to make their lives more exciting and to make themselves feel more important and lively. For the same reason, people join associations—because associations offer more opportunities for conflict, and also because the association has all the "important" political positions that the larger political system has. In each association someone gets to be President, or military chief, treasurer, loyal follower, mistreated follower, and so on. In countries where new associations are relatively easy to form, one will probably find more variation between the larger political system and the political associations, because people can express their imaginations and wishes more in groups that are not so limited by the real world.

Very often, people get involved in political associations to salvage their pride. (This is not to deny that they *also* join associations to promote worthy causes, get results, and find company.) Belonging to exclusive groups and becoming Grand Dragon (or whatever) helps some people recover their *self-esteem*. Otherwise they think they are looked down upon and losing out. If people like this become leaders, they are likely to be bad losers and to try desperately to avoid further humiliations and mortification by making it look as if they are never to blame, even though that means being hard on others and finding scapegoats. On the other hand, such desperate (so-called ambitious) people provide a lot of energy for the political system; they jump at every chance to do something meritorious (or, anyhow, *no*torious); and they provoke new conflicts which make the political system more exciting.

When a bum or alcoholic stops you on the street and asks for money, you may give it to him because (1) you feel sorry for him, (2) he might injure you otherwise, and/or (3) you feel a little inflated since, by comparison with him, you are so rich and so good. *Or* you may refuse because (1) you are afraid of him and want to get out of there, (2) you disapprove of the whole system of private enterprise by beggars, and/or (3) you feel a little inflated since, by comparison with him, you are so rich and so good that you do not have to deal with such lowly creatures at all. Likewise, there are politicians who act like the beggar (getting others to feel sorry for them, to save them from their loneliness or starvation, to give them their just desserts, to reject them as they deserve, or to join them in the gutter by playing the "sucker"). And there are politicians who play the "donor" part—who prove (in the face of so many doubts?) that they are awfully kind and good; who rescue their poor constituents; who give in to criminal threats; who impose economies and hardships on the followers for their own good; and who treat the naughty ones firmly and put them in their rightful (lowly) places. Most politicians play both parts, and it is most difficult to see through the resulting smoke-screens. The whole thing could be avoided if people were not made to feel so bad in the first place and if the government (or someone) provided more interesting things for bums and alcoholics to do. The fact is that bumming around is what lots of people are most skillful at; they are experts at it after a while, and, what's more, they are afraid of other things they could be doing with their time. Politics is one way of spending time and one way of testing whether other people think some-one is as bad or as exalted as he himself thinks.

Careers in politics offer a unique combination of opportuni-ties: great power *plus* much publicity. One might expect, then, that a political career would be irresistibly attractive to people who crave both attention and power. Since people seek power to "get even" with the world, intimidate others, and feel important, and since they seek attention when they feel neglected, left out, or looked down upon, there is some risk that the political career will appeal to anti-social characters.

Even when the aims of an association appear innocent and non-political, government officials can get awfully jumpy about them. Up until recent times, governments have been suspicious of private associations because of their potential for becoming conspiracies to overthrow the government. The larger the number of people who get together in a group, the more trouble they can be to the rulers if they start making demands or threats. In the Roman Empire, for example, only burial societies and religious fraternities were permitted to organize. Families, churches, work groups, and so on, have been responsible for many of the feuds and civil wars of time past. And only in the last few hundred years have rulers dared to tolerate all sorts of political associations; in most parts of the world, they still do not.

This fear of conspiracies helps explain why some political systems require all associations to be "semi-official" branches of the government and why other political systems give a lot of publicity to private associations and are nervous and critical about *secret* societies. Interestingly enough, in many countries the government itself is a secret society; and in some tribal societies the warriors all belong to "secret" societies or "lodges" much like the military elites of our own society.

When associations are not formed primarily to affect the external world or to strengthen the opinions of like-minded members of the general public, one can think of them as MICROPOLITICAL SYSTEMS. Each such association has its own system of authority-relations, conflicts, decision rules, and representation. When a micropolitical system is closely linked with the larger political system, one says that it is a *subsystem*. When it has little or no effect on the larger system, one can regard it as an independent micropolitical system. For instance, a hypothetical group like the Lithuanian Marxist Study Group, if it never runs anybody for office and does not have a noticeable effect on the opinions of people outside the group, might just as well be thought of as an independent micropolitical system.

On the other hand, when associations are formed for the purpose of imitating certain aspects of a real social system, they are called SIMULATIONS. Simulations can be done by having real people play the positions within the group or by having computers imitate the typical behavior of these people. (The computer would, of course, have to be directed, or programmed, by the person running the simulation so that it would only be reflecting that person's ideas of how the real system works.) Simulations of political systems and their subsystems can be used to teach students how the system works, to test theories of how it works, and to get new ideas of how it works.

The difference between political systems and their subsystems is a *relative* one. And one can think of nations as being subsystems of the international political system; one can think of states as subsystems of the United States; one can think of the

United Nations as a subsystem of the nations "belonging" to it (i.e., to which *it* belongs); or one can think of the federal government as a subsystem (as an agent) of the communities that make up the country. It is customary, however, to think of B as the subsystem if one believes that A controls or commands B.

Sample Theorem

By joining a political association, a person can reduce the amount of power he has in the political system.

Proof

(i) People have different wants at different times (Assumption 3).

(ii) Therefore, there is some chance that the members of any political association will fall into conflict among themselves (Implication and *def.* Conflict).

(iii) The more of their energy people spend on the conflict within the group, the less they have to spend on the rest of the political system (Assumption 8).

(iv) Each member of a political association had some quantity of energy before joining the association (Assumptions 1, 6, and 8, and Sample Theorem Ch. 2).

(v) If the amount of power a person *gained* by joining the association is (at some point in time) *less* than the amount he is spending on the conflicts within the association, he has reduced the amount of political power he has (Steps iii and iv). (Or, to generalize: it is possible for associations to weaken and deadlock a political system.)

Sample Theorem

If people firmly believe something to be so, they will act as if it were so, and their behavior will be so whether the thing itself actually is or is not so (W. I. Thomas' law: originally stated as; "If men define situations as real they are real in their consequences.")

Corollary

If people believe a particular individual or association to have lots of power, they will act as if that were true and will avoid any test of whether it is true.

Proof

(i) Opinions are what people tell one another about the world, and therefore what people know or believe they know about the political world is partly what they have been told by others (*Ex def.* Opinion).

(ii) People have to believe *something(s)* about the world, or else they could not survive in it; that is, people have to decide which of the opinions they hear they want to take seriously and act upon (Assumptions 1 and 6).

(iii) Every act implies a decision, because some alternatives (including inaction) have been abandoned (*Ex def.* Decision).

(iv) Every act (e.g., voting for Senator X) can be done for a *number* of different reasons; but the same act is the same, regardless of the reasons for which it stands (Assumption 2).

(v) Therefore, since the act can stand for many things and yet be the same act, the reasons for the act can be true or false, imaginary or real, and still result in the same act.

Sample Theorem

People who avoid belonging to associations do so because they want to belong to associations (Kant's paradox).

Proof

(i) All people have some things they would like to do and have not done (Assumption 1).

(ii) People who form associations are able to do things they otherwise could not do (*Ex def.* and previous Theorems).

(iii) People avoid associations either because they are not allowed to join or because, once they belong to an association, they find they cannot do what they wanted to do (Assumptions 3 and 4).

(iv) Thus, to be able to do what they could not do without joining an association, people quit associations or avoid joining them. OR, people who do not belong to political associations do so because they cannot find the kind of association that will get them what they want.

Problems

1. Many associations, and certainly the largest and most powerful ones, have leaders or officials who are paid to do the day-to-day work of the associations. Leaders of important associations have lots of the things that people want—power, high salaries, prestige. At the same time, many of the *members* (the rank-and-file) of the same association may have very little power, money, or prestige. Representative examples might include a labor union, a civil rights association, or a political party. You can see that in these circumstances the leaders might want to do something that would maintain their own social position but that would not be in the best interests of the membership. Assess the consequences of this fact in light of the above discussion of associations and especially with regard to the Theorems.

2. Some people argue that associations cannot be democratic in the sense discussed in Chapter 7. This fact stems, it is said, from the "iron law of oligarchy" which holds that all associations of whatever sort at any point in history are ruled by a few people who (1) select their own successors, (2) make decisions in their own interest, (3) try to deceive the membership that what they (the leaders) are doing is for the good of the members when it really is not, and (4) eliminate, by a variety of means, any group in the association that tries to change things or wants to get a new set of officials in office. Why might this be so (if in fact it is)? You may find it useful to re-read the Theorems and the discussion of conflict in Chapter 4 before answering this question.

3. All associations contain factions. This is so, in part, because people are not willing to let everybody have the same

amount of say over the activities of the association: they may have also found out that by forming cliques in the organization they may get more power than someone else. Consider an association with 1,000 members that is called upon to vote "for" or "against" a certain person who wants to be the president of the association. In a random vote (such as might occur if no one had talked to anyone else about the election), 500 people would vote "for" and 500 people would vote "against." But assume that one member talked to 49 others about the election. They might form a clique in order to control the election. How might they proceed?

4. If you were a member of an association that had divided into a majority and a minority faction and you happened to be a member of the minority, you might find out that all the decisions being made by the association were ones that you did not like. Assume also that you had talked to all the members of the majority and tried to convince them that they should join your side but they had all refused. (Perhaps they were very obstinate people!) You might want to quit the association because there seems to be no chance of your "winning." However, suppose that you could *expand the size* of the association by getting new people to join who would take your side. Now *you* might be in the majority because you have controlled the "scope of conflict," and he who controls the scope of conflict "controls the outcome." What may your opponents do in response? Do you see now one of the reasons why organizations try to recruit new members? If you are interested in the development of the Democratic and Republican parties and their expansion, you may find it useful to think about the "scope of conflict" theory.

5. It has been said that a successful political party in Canada must secure support from at least two of the country's five regions: the Atlantic provinces, Quebec, Ontario, the Prairies, or British Columbia. If this is the case, would you expect the two largest regions or some other combination of regions to form a *coalition* to exploit the other regions who are not necessary to form a winning coalition? What has actually happened in Canada?

6. A few years ago the Federal Power Commission let a

private corporation build dams at the Hell's Canyon site on the Snake River. Some people in the region opposed this decision because they believed that natural resources should not be exploited for private profit; others opposed it because the dams would flood their grazing lands; others, because they favored another plan which (they said) would be better for flood control, irrigation, and the migrating fish (salmon and sturgeon). (a) What does this Chapter suggest the opposition might have done? What would be the pros and cons of doing it? (b) Regulatory agencies like the FPC have to work closely with the people they regulate, and often individuals are put on the regulatory agency *because* they are experienced in the regulated business. What evidence would you want before concluding that a regulatory agency is "captured" by or has become a part of the regulated group?

7. It is sometimes said that political groups, such as the Anti-Saloon League or the National Association for the Advancement of Colored People, have purposes and that the more effective groups are single-purpose groups. Is it possible for a political group to have a purpose? If so, give an example.

8. What if the content analysis of thousands of speeches by dozens of political leaders in Country X over the past 50 years showed beyond a reasonable doubt that the winners consistently used the pronoun "we" more often than the losers, and the losers consistently used the pronoun "you" more than the winners, thus:

	Average Use Of We, Our, Ours, or Us, Per 1000 Words	Average Use of You, Your, or Yours, Per 1000 Words
Winners	5.8	1.3
Losers	0.7	8.0

Assume that Country X is now ruled by the sick and elderly General Gross, that all the experts agree that he will be succeeded either by Colonel Latke or by Colonel Matzos, and that a content analysis of the speeches of the colonels over the past 16 months shows:

	Average Use of We, Our, Ours, or Us, Per 1000 Words	Average Use of You, Your, or Yours, Per 1000 Words
Latke	3.1	0.2
Matzos	1.5	9.3

What conclusions, if any, would you draw about the question of who is likely to succeed General Gross? How confident would you be about your prediction? Give the reasons for your conclusions and for your level of confidence.

Suggested Readings

Herbert Agar, *The Price of Union* (1950).

Arthur Bentley, *The Process of Government* (1908).

Maurice Duverger, *Political Parties* (1955).

Sigmund Freud, *Group Psychology and the Analysis of the Ego* (1922).

Morton Fried, *Evolution of Political Societies* (1967).

Harold D. Lasswell, "Faction," in *Encyclopedia of the Social Sciences,* Vol. 5, p. 49 (1930).

Seymour M. Lipset, M. Trow, and J. Coleman, *Union Democracy* (1956).

James March and Herbert Simon, *Organizations* (1958).

Robert Michels, *Political Parties* (1915).

INDEX

Abrahamson, Mark, 29
Achilles, 73
Affirmation, 5
Agar, Herbert, 107
Agency, 85 ff
Agents, 45, 47, 85 ff
Agger, Robert, 93
Anarchists, 43
Anarchy, 88
Anomie (*see* Non-participation)
Apprenticeship, 48, 71
Aquinas, St. Thomas, 76
Arbitration, 59
Aristocracy, 88
Aristotle, 29
Aron, Raymond, 54
Arrow's paradox, 51
Association, 23–24, 49, 95 ff
Assumptions 1, 3–6
Authority, 1, 8
Autocracy, 88

Bacon, Francis, 93
Bandwagon effect, 67

Basic human nature, 3–4
Beatles, 87
Behavior
    dysfunctional, 18
    functional, 18
Bellamy, Edward, 63
Benedict, Ruth, 83
Benefits, 15
Bentley, Arthur, 107
Bolsheviks, 12
Boulding, Kenneth E., 54, 63, 83
Braybrooke, David, 39
Brokers, 72
Bruck, H., 39
Buchanan, James M., 29
Buddha, 73
Bureaucracy (*see* Structure; Rules)
Burke, Edmund, 93
Buss, A. H., 54

Caesar, Julius, 73
Campaigns (*see* Support)
Campbell, Angus, 83
Capitulation, 56

Caruso, Enrico, 87
Caste, 21
Causes, intended-unintended, viii
Change, 10–13
Chase, Stuart, 6
Citizenship, vii–viii
Civil Disobedience, 58
Class, social, 21–22
Cliques, 96, 105
Coleman, James, 107
Communism, 8, 69
Comparability, 5
Complexity (of propaganda), 74–75
Compromise, 56–57
Conflict, 13, 31, 40–54, 69
  closed, 45
  open, 45–46
Conflict-avoidance, 55
Conflict-resolution, 55–64
Congress, U.S., 17, 18, 21, 25
Consensus, 22, 69
Conservatives, 43
Constitutions, 13, 42
Consultation, 88–90
Content analysis, 106
Contract, 43–44
Convention (vs. Nature), 3–4
Converse, Philip, 83
Conversion, political, 69
Cooperation, 13, 44
Costs, 15
Credenda, 57, 66
Crises, 9
Crusades, 44
Curry, Robert, 29
Custom, 10

Dahl, Robert A., 39, 93
Dawson, R., 83
Deception, 44
Decision, 30–39
  comprehensive, 33 ff
  fragmented, 33 ff
  inaction as, 30
  incremental, 33 ff
  integrated, 33 ff
  latitude, 31–32
  political, 31
Definitions, viii
DeGaulle, Charles, 87
Democracy, 88, 92, 93
Deutsch, Karl, 83

Dewey, John, 6
Discontinuity, 5–6
Distribution
  cumulative, 46
  uneven, 46
Downs, Anthony, 29
Duverger, Maurice, 107
Dysfunctional (behavior), 18

Easton, David, 29
Edelman, Murray, 84
Elections (see Agency; Opinion)
Elites, 25–26, 73–74
Empiricism, x
Energy, human, 6
Entropy, 96–97
Equilibrium, 10–13, 15
Exchange theory, 14 ff
Excommunication, 72
Exodus, 41, 75

Factions, 96, 104–105
Faking, 44
Fate control, 56–57
Foreign policy, 10
Frank, Lawrence, 6
Franklin, Benjamin, 20
Freedom, 67, 77
Freud, Sigmund, 54, 107
Fried, Morton, 107
Friedrich, Carl J., 39
Fromm, Erich, 84
Functional (behavior), 18
Functionalism (see Structural-
  functional analysis)
Functions
  latent, 18–19
  manifest, 18

Games
  mixed-motive, 14
  zero-sum, 13
Game theory, 13 ff
Gandhi, M. K., 54
George, Alexander, 93
George, Juliette, 93
Goals, 4
God, 42, 65, 76
Goldrich, Daniel, 93
Goldwater, Barry, 13
Groups, 21, 49, 96
  (see also Associations)

Heidenkeimer, Arnold, 39
Heller, Joseph, 78
Heroes, 73
Hirschman, Albert, 29
Hitler, Adolph, 34, 75
Hobbes, Thomas, 54
House of Representatives, U.S., 5
Hunter, Floyd, 94
Hyman, Herbert, 84

Identification, 49
Ideology, 8, 41–42, 68–69, 88
Idols, 86–87
Iklé, Fred Charles, 63
Iliad, 41
Illusions, 40
Inaction, 30, 40
Incas, 11–12
Indecision, 40
Individuality, 5
Information, 2, 32, 34 ff, 89
Institutions (*see* Structure)
Interactions, 17
Interest groups (*see* Groups)
Iron law of oligarchy, 104
Irresponsibility, 58

Janis, Irving L., 39
Jehovah, 41, 75
John XXIII, 64
Johnson, Lyndon B., 13
Johnston, R. E., 84

Kant, Immanuel, 64
Kant's paradox, 103
Kaplan, Abraham, 6
Kariel, Henry, 94
Kecskemeti, Paul, 64
Kelley, Stanley, 84
Key, V. O., Jr., 84
Kluckhohn, Clyde, 84
Kolko, Gabriel, 54

Lady Godiva, 4
Lall, Arthur, 64
Lane, Robert, 84
Lasswell, Harold D., v–vi, 54, 84, 97, 107
Las Vegas, 5
Law, 73, 76
Leadership, 66, 72–73, 85 ff, 97–98
Learning, 67–68

Legitimacy (*see* Rules; Support; Ideology)
Leighton, Alexander, 94
Leviticus, viii
Lewin, Kurt, 64
Liberals, 43
Liberty, 76–77
Liddell-Hart, B. H., 54
Lindblom, Charles E., 39
Lipset, S. M., 84, 107
Locke, John, 64
Lorenz, Konrad, 54
Loyalty, 87
Luttberg, Norman, 84
Lynd, Robert S., 6

Machiavelli, Niccolo, 54
MacIntosh, Donald, 6
MacLeish, Archibald, 82
Madison, James, 29
Mao Tse-tung, 87
March, James, 107
Markets, 15
Marx, Karl, 22, 54
Masses, 74
Matthew, viii
Matthews, Donald, 94
Mead, Margaret, 64
Mediation, 59
Merriam, Charles, 66, 84
Merton, Robert, 20, 29
Michels, Robert, 107
Milbrath, Lester, 94
Mill, John Stuart, 94
Miller, Warren, 83
Mills, C. Wright, 29
Mitchell, William C., 29
Miranda, 57, 66
Mobility, 21
Monarchy, 88
Moral questions, viii
More, Thomas, 64
Mortification, 71
Moses, 75–76
Mystification, 57, 75
Myth (*see* Ideology)

Napoleon, 73
Nature (vs. Convention), 3–4
Non-participation, 58
Norms, 52
North Atlantic Treaty Organization, 44

Oligarchy, 88
Opinion, 65 ff
  leaders (*see* Leadership)
  polls, 65, 79–80, 92
Otto the Great, 12
Overlapping membership, 24

Parsons, Talcott, 20
Parties, political, 96, 98
Payoffs, 73
Peace, 43
Personalities, 52, 87
Pharaoh, 41
Plato, 29
Pluralism, 23 ff
Policy, 68
  public, 15
  foreign, 10
Political science (def.), 1
Pope, 8
Poseidon, 41
Power, 23 ff, 35, 97
  perceived, 98
  political, 97
Preferences, 30–31, 35, 46
President 16, 31, 43, 57–58, 66, 92
Prewitt, K., 83
Price, Leontyne, 86
Principal, 85
Prisoner's Dilemma, 14
Privacy, 58
Propaganda, 74 ff
Property, 76
Public Interest (*see* Agency; Representation)
Pye, Lucian, 29

Rank, Otto, 94
Rapoport, Anatol, 54
Rational decision-making, 35–36
Regime, 96
Representation, 88
  (*see also* Agency)
Rescuers, 87
Resources, political, 46
Revolution, 58
Revolutionaries, 43
Reynolds v. *Sims,* 93
Right, 9
Richardson, L., 54
Rites of passage, 72
Roman Empire, 12, 100
Romeo, 41

Roosevelt, Theodore, 65
Routines, 30
Rulers, 88
Rules, 3, 8, 24, 42, 43
Rumpelstiltzkin, 73

Sampson, 73
Sapin, B., 39
Schattschneider, E. E., 54
Schattschneider's law, 59, 60
Schelling, Thomas, 54
Schilling, Warner R., 39
Schumpeter's dictum, vii
Scientific method, 1–2
Scope of conflict, 105
Sears, David, 84
Sedition, 63
Self-esteem, 87, 99
Selznick, Philip, 64
Set, 7
Shakespeare, William, 54
Simmel, Georg, 54
Simon, Herbert, 39, 107
Simplicity (of propaganda), 75
Simulations, 101
Situation, viii
Skill, 48
Sklar, Judith, 39
Slogans, 53–54
Snyder, Richard C., 39
Sociability, 5
Socialization, 12, 28, 68, 71
Sorel, Georges, 54
Specialization, 87
Spitz, Rene, 6
Spokesman, 72
Stability (*see* Equilibrium)
Stalemate, 59
Stokes, D., 83
Strickland, D. A., 39, 64, 84
Structural-functional analysis, 17–21
Structure, 17
Subsystems, 101–102
Support, 15, 73
Supreme Court, U.S., 25, 69, 93
Swanson, B., 93
Symbolism, 4
System, 7
  international political, 9–10
Systems
  binary, 7–8
  micropolitical, 101

political, 7, 8–10, 76
social, 8

Teleology, 19
Theorems, ix
Theories, partial, 10–24
Theory, 2–4
    elite, 23–26
    exchange, 14–17
    game, 13–14
    moral, 22 ff
    pluralist, 23–26
Thomas, W. I., 72, 102
Thoreau, Henry David, 78
Time, 46–48
Training, 71
Treaties, 10
Trotsky, Lev, 72
Trouble, 49
Trow, M., 107
Truman, Harry, 16, 39
Tullock, Gordon, 29
Tybalt, 41

United Nations, 10, 102

Values, 5, 52
Veblen, Thorstein, 64
Violence, 41, 48–49
Vischer, Theodor, viii
Voting, 5, 15, 31
    (see also Agency)

Wade, L. L., 29
Wants, viii, 9, 26–27, 60–61
War, 9–10, 41, 45–46
Warner, W. Lloyd, 29
Warsaw Pact, 44
Williams, J. D., 54
Wohlstetter, Roberta, 84
Wright, Quincy, 54

Zald, Mayer, 29
Zeus, 41
Zipf, H., 68–84